# Angk

## 20 Must See Temples

*By Anton Swanepoel*

# AntonSwanepoel
## www.antonswanepoelbooks.com

All pictures are property of

*Anton Swanepoel*

*http://antonswanepoelbooks.com/*
*http://antonswanepoelbooks.com/blog/*
*http://www.facebook.com/AuthorAntonSwanepoel*
*https://twitter.com/Author_Anton*

# Table of Contents

Make your trip to Angkor Wat special by journaling your trip in an Angkor Wat Journal. 100 pages each with a different picture of Angkor Wat or another temple.

### Available Journals

- Collage Ruled Journal
- Non-ruled Journal
- Dream Journal
- Gratitude Journal

**http://antonswanepoelbooks.com/angkor_wat_journals.php**

# *Introduction*

Magical Angkor Wat temple amazes over 2 million visitors each year. However, there are more than 700 temples scattered around Angkor Wat and the nearby mountains and towns, with more than 70 temples and sights in the Angkor Archaeological Park alone (Angkor Wat Temple is situated in the Angkor Archaeological Park). This book gives 22 of the best temples.

Angkor Archaeological Park stretches over 400 square km and contains some of the most magnificent temple remains of several capitals of the Khmer Empire. The park is around 5km from the nearby town, Siem Reap, and was declared a UNESCO World Heritage site in 1992. Both Buddhism and Hindu temples are found within the park, with many altered from Buddhism to Hindu and then back again. When Jayavarman II declared himself God-King, and World-Emperor in 802 in the Kulen Mountains, he started the rise of one of the greatest South East Asian empires of the ancient era. The Angkor area continued to grow through the times, until 1431, when a rebellion led by Ayutthaya sacked Angkor, and caused the population to abandon the temples in 1432. During the time, the capital moved from in order: Banteay Chhmar, Kulen Mountains, Roluos Group temples, Angkor, Koh Ker Temple Site, Angkor, Banteay Samre, Angkor, and lastly to Phnom Penh

Make your travels smoother, get by book 100 International Travel tips. **https://amzn.to/2poKvVt**

If you are backpacking, get my book Backpacking SouthEast Asia. **https://amzn.to/2Dfosuk**
If you are thinking of motorcycling, get my book, Motorbiking Cambodia & Vietnam. **https://amzn.to/2NVRqU4**

Be prepared, get 50 facts you should know when visiting Cambodia. **https://amzn.to/2xZlnZq**

## *How To Get To Siem Reap*

Siem Reap is the gateways city for Angkor and does have an international airport. You can also fly internationally to Phnom Penh, the capital of Cambodia. There is no accommodation at Angkor, so you have to stay in Siem Reap.

**From International** you often fly first into Phnom Penh and then to Siem Reap. Most flights from America or Japan land in Malaysia on the way. Often it is cheaper to fly to Bangkok and take a bus to Siem Reap. Visas are available on arrival at the Siem Reap and Phnom Penh airports. You can get an online visa that works at most borders. **https://www.evisa.gov.kh/**. *For visa on arrival, you need four passport photos.* Good flight search engines are **https://www.momondo.com/**, and **https://www.skyscanner.net/**.

**From** Bangkok by land to Siem Reap is around 8 hours by bus. You would normally cross at the Poipet border. Make sure your bus ticket is for all the way to Siem Reap else you will need to hire a taxi at the border. Poipet border has visa on arrival.

**From Vietnam** if you are in Saigon, you would first go to Phnom Penh though the Bavet border. Around 4 hours. Then take an 8 hours bus ride from Phnom Penh to Siem Reap. From Hanoi in Vietnam, you would need to enter the top part of Cambodia and come all the way down. This is a very long ride with not very good busses. Rather fly to Siem Reap. Bavet border has visa on arrival.

**From** Sihanoukville, Kampot, or Kep, you will first take a bus ride to Phnom Penh, around 4 hours, then a bus ride to Siem Reap. Overnight buses taking around 13 hours is available, but not recommended.
**Tip:** Two of the better bus companies to use are **http://catmekongexpress.com/** and **http://www.giantibis.com/**.

## *Siem Reap Accommodation*

Siem Reap is the capital city of Siem Reap Province in northwestern Cambodia, and the gateway city to Angkor Wat. The city's name translates to "Defeat of Siam". According to legend, King Ang Chan (1516–1566) gave the city its name after he drove back an army sent to invade Cambodia by the Thai King Maha Chakkraphat in 1549. This has not been proven as fact as of yet and remains a legend and the actual origin of the name remains unknown.

Today, Siem Reap is a vibrant town and a favorite destination of travelers seeking to experience the mystery of Angkor Wat. One of the most know streets in Siem Reap is Pub Street, where a variety of shops, restaurants, a market, and more can be found. Siem Reap city is mostly a cluster of small villages along the Siem Reap River, with modern shops mostly situated around Sivutha Street and the Psar Chas area (Old Market area). The Wat Bo area became a popular place for guesthouses and restaurants while across the river, the Psar Leu area developed into a large market. Siem Reap is a mix between the modern shops of Phnom Penh and the laid back rustic atmosphere of Battambang.

Guide to shopping places and markets in Siem Reap, Gift For You.
*http://www.antonswanepoelbooks.com/shopping_in_siem_reap.php*

Accommodation range from backpacker shared rooms for $3 a night, to $10 rooms with an air-conditioner and up to $400 a night in luxury hotel rooms with your own driver and car to take you to the temples. **https://www.expedia.com/** offers upper to mid-range accommodations while
**https://www.booking.com/index.en-gb.html** offers mid to budget accommodations, **https://www.hostelworld.com/**, the names says it all.

## *Transport To Angkor Wat Temple*

Siem Reap is about 5 Km from the entry to Angkor Wat Park. It takes about 15 minutes by tuk-tuk to get to the entry gate. The outer circuit is around 21 km with the inner circuit round 17 km. Walking or jogging to the temples is not a viable option.

### Bicycles

Most backpacker hotels rent out bicycles for around $1 a day or give them for free if you stay with the hotel. This allows you to go at your own pace and be able to walk around temples. Make sure the bicycle is in a good condition before you take it. If you do get a flat tire, just look for small shops that hang motorcycle tires out by the road, they will be able to fix your tire for a few Riel (less than a $1). If you get tired, hire a tuk-tuk and put the bicycle in the tuk-tuk. This is often done when travelers are tired and want to easily return at night from Angkor.

Tip: Take a headlamp with if to plan to see the sunset at Angkor. There are no street lamps when you come back.

Warning: Always lock your bicycle up no matter where you leave it.

### Electric Assisted Bicycle

You can hire an electric assisted bicycle for around $10 a day. It is a bit faster than a bicycle, but you still have to pedal. There are charging points all over Angkor. Note that the range is around 40km and max speed around 20km/h. At $10 a day, if you are two people, it is cheaper to rent a Tuk-tuk for the day. See **http://www.greene-bike.com/**

### Motorcycle Taxi

Motorcycle taxis are a cheap option, but can be dangerous. Often it is just a local that wants to make a few extra bucks. So don't be shocked when an army general or police officer offers you a ride. Some are actually guides and you can get a good deal. Prices are around $10 for a day. Mostly you would use them just to go a short distance around town, for $1 or so. Hiring of motorcycles in Siem Reap is illegal but done. Do so at your own risk.

**Warning:** Always wear a helmet and hold on tightly. Most of the guys cannot ride properly and accidents to happen.

### Tuk-Tuks

Tuk-tuks are the most popular transport at Angkor. They are more comfortable and safer than a motorcycle, but cheaper than a car. You can fit around 4 or so people in a tuk-tuk. A tuk-tuk is a small open carriage that is drawn behind a motorcycle. You pay for the tuk-tuk and not per person. Prices are from around $15 to $25 for the day depending on if you want to see the sunrise and sunset. You can hire them to go to Kulen and Koh Ker Temples. Always arrange the price beforehand. If you change the route, the prices changes as well.

**Tip:** The tuk-tuks that hang around hotels and shopping centers are more expensive. So are those that your hotel call. Just walk a bit down the street and you will find loads on street corners. Get one for multiple days and you can get a discount.

### Private Cars and Taxis

If you cannot stand the heat, then hiring a car with an air conditioner is a good option. It can also be cheap if you go with a group. Normally cars are around $30 a day, so split between 4 is not bad. Your hotel can arrange a driver or go to any of the travel agencies all around Siem Reap. You can book online, here is one site, **https://bookmebus.com/en**

## *Angkor Wat Tickets*

**All visitors to the park must have a photo id entry pass that is issued at the office just before entering the park.** Note that most temples close to the park, such as Banteay Srei, Banteay Samre, and the Roluos group, require you to have an Angkor Pass. Thus, if you want to visit these temples, get your pass before you head out to the temples. Outer temples such as Koh Ker, and Ben Mealea, have their own entry pass office. Do note that the rules do change without notice, so it is advised to ask your tuk tuk driver for requirements before you head out. The office for tickets to Angkor Wat Park is on Charles De Gualle Street, 2.8km from the crossing with national road 6.

**GPS For Ticket Office:** 13°23'12.7"N 103°51'50.6"E.
$72 for 7 entries, valid for one month.
$62 for 3 entries, valid for one week.
$37 for a day pass. You can only buy a day pass for the next day after 5pm. Children under 12 years old are free. Children under 12 years old are free. If they have their passport with them.
**Open:** 5:00am ~ 5:30pm for tickets. 5:30am ~ 5:30pm for temples. Phnom Bakheng and Pre Rup temple close at 7pm.

### Keep You Ticket Safe

Even after entering the main park, you will need to show your ticket at every temple.

**Notice:** Children under 12 cannot go up to the central tower of Angkor Wat Temple.

**Tip:** Buy your ticket for the next day the evening before at 5pm and then go see the sunset for free. That way you save time getting your ticket in the morning and get to see some temples for free.

**Warning:** Only Cash is accepted, there is an ATM at the office.

## *Tips For Making The Most Of Your Visit*

If you have time, it is a good idea to visit the Angkor National Museum first to discover some history of the temples, Khmer Empire as well as see a video of the sun rising over Angkor Wat.

**Warning:** DO NOT DRINK THE TAP WATER, you may get violently ill. Brush your teeth with bottled water and close your mouth in the shower.

### Get Up Early

Access to the park is from 5:30 am and the ticket office opens at 5. It gets hot all year round in Cambodia, and the park is huge with temples sometimes km's (miles) from one another. You need all the time you can get to make the best of your visit.

### Spend At Least 3 Days at The Park

Temples were built from around 611 to around 1307, and were dedicated to different religions and gods. They are all unique. With so many temples to see and appreciate, take the time to explore them properly.

### Plan What Temples To Visit Beforehand

Use the included map, GPS locations as well as suggested itinerary to make the best of your time. Know what your aim for the day is, and plan accordingly.

**Large Temples:** Angkor Wat, Baphuon, Bayon, Phnom Bakheng, and Pre Rup.
**Jungle like Temples:** Ta Phnom, Preah Kan, and Ta Som, are partially overgrown and give the Tomb Raider feeling.
**Temples With Bas Reliefs:** Angkor Wat, Bayon.
**Temples With Intricate Art:** Banteay Srei Temple.
**Top 5 Temples To See:** Angkor Wat, Bayon, Ta Prohm, Banteay Srei, and Ta Som.

## Wear Bright Colored Clothing

Many of the images you take will have a dark background as many of the temples are shrouded in forest canopy as well as the temples are dark themselves. If you wear dark clothing, you will blend into the background. Good colors to wear are white, yellow, light blue and pink or strong red. This allows you to stand out against the forest on pictures.

## Eat At The Temples

Going back to your hotel to have breakfast or lunch is extra taxi fare as well as a wastes of time. You can eat at the temples from either traditional Khmer restaurants or more upmarket restaurants just by the entrance of Angkor Wat. You can also ask your hotel to make you a to-go lunch or get some snacks from the convenient stores the evening before. Water and sodas are sold all over Angkor. They are a bit more expensive than bringing your own, but are cold.

## What To Wear

In the cooler months it can still go into the 30 degree centigrade and in the summer months in the low 40s. Wear comfortable light clothing that covers at least your knees and shoulders. We highly suggest you get a long sleeve shirt and pants from the local markets as the sun can burn you badly. These are light and cool. Do use sunscreen. Wear a hat and possibly sun glasses. For shoes, trainers or sneakers are fine. Light trail or hiking shoes are better. Flip flops, sandals and high heels are not recommended. Open feet, sweat, and sand, not a good mix.

**Warning:** You have to **cover up your knees and shoulders** with a fixed item of clothing. Meaning you cannot throw a scarf over a tank top to try to cover your shoulders. You will not be allowed into the inner parts of Angkor Wat. You have to remove all head covering at the inner part of Angkor Wat.

### Go From North To South

Many visitors leave Angkor at around 6:30 to 7am after the sunrise, to eat breakfast. This is a good time to explore Angkor Wat while it is cool and there are fewer people around. The crowds normally return around 9 to 10am. Tours go from Angkor Wat and then slowly make their way up to the northern temples. You can skip most of the crowd if you go directly after Angkor Wat to the south gate, then up to the northern temples like Preah Kan and work your way down. If you can stand the heat, from 12 to around 2pm the temples are mostly empty. From 3 to 4pm the heat is less and the lighting is better for taking pictures.

### Angkor Wat And Kids

Angkor Wat Temple are not for all kids. Children under 12 cannot go up the central part of the temple. The area is large and small kids may get tired. Viewing temples is also mostly in the sun, and kids can get sunburn and dehydrated very easily. Do prepare for this. The terrain is from large broken stones, steep steps, big tree roots, to narrow pathways. It is not pram friendly. If you have small kids then a baby carrier is best. There are no playgrounds or things to do for kids in Angkor Wat, so they may get bored. If you plan on being out all day, take something to keep them distracted while you do temple hopping. It can get very crowded at Angkor, especially at sunrise. Keep a close watch on your kids.

### Apsara Dancers

There are often Apsara dancer at Bayon temple on the top level. You can get a free viewing at Temple Balcony Bar in Pub Street with dinner (7:30pm).

## *Angkor Wat Sunrise and Sunset Guide*

Following are some tips and advice for enjoying the sunrise and sunset, and getting some good images.

### What Time Of Year To Go

To get the sun directly behind the central pillar you need to be there at vernal or autumnal equinox. March 21 – 22 and 23 September. If you are not there at those times, the sun will come up either left or right of the towers. You can move around to align the sun and the towers. Sunrise go from around 5.30am in June to around 6.30am in January. In January you can capture photos of Angkor Wat Temple with star trails as a backdrop.

**Tip:** Different times of the year affects the lighting. In the first few months the skies are generally cloudless. However, the air is not clear and due to haze (especially in March, April, and May) the sun will appear as a big red ball. At the start of the monsoon season, there will be clouds and often you may not be able to see the sun. However, the clouds add a dramatic effect to your pictures. If you can get an open shot of the sun after rains, the sunrises will be spectacular. October to March is best.

### Buy Your Tickets The day Before

Even though the ticket office opens at 5am, you will want to get your ticket the evening before, or use a multiday pass. When you are buying your ticket, others that have their tickets are lining up already for the best seating spot at Angkor Wat.

### Check The Weather

During the dry season (November to April) you don't have to worry much. But for the rest of the year do check that it will not be an overcast or rainy day between 4am and 7am. See https://www.wunderground.com. You can sign up for daily forecasts by email.

### Get To Angkor Wat Temple Early

This goes hand in hand with buying your ticket the day before. You want to leave your hotel at 4:45am or earlier. To get a good spot, you need to be one of the first when the gates open at 5am. Especially in the high season.

### Best Places To Stand At Angkor Wat

Where to stand depends on what time of the year you go. For starters, you want to be behind the left water pool as you come in. However, you may want to move to the far left or far right of the pool to get the sun aligned. The middle of the pool should be fine for the equinox. After the vernal equinox in March, the sun starts to come up more to the left side of the towers. You want to move to the right to align the shot. By June the sun will be the furthest to the left so try the right edge of the pool. Then the sun moves to the right again until it comes up behind the towers in September again.

After September the sun starts to rise more to the right of the central tower. Here you want to move to the left of the pool. By December the sun will rise the furthest right so try the far left of the pool. Then the sun starts to move left until March when it is behind the towers again.

### Bonus Tips

- To get the sun and temple reflecting in the pool, find a spot with limited lily pads in front of you. Also stand as close to the water as possible to prevent someone from pushing in front of you and blocking your shot. If there are rocks in the water, avoid standing behind them as people will jump on them and stand in front of you.
- If it is not essential to get the sun over the central pillar or it is a bit cloudy, go to the pool on the right. It is far less crowded and the view is almost as good.

- If you have a ticket, tell your driver to take the old road. It is Charles de Gaulle and it runs north-south from the southern side of the moat. This way you will get the Angkor faster.
- Take a headlamp (flashlight), insect repellent, snacks and something to drink. It can be a 2 hour wait. Ask your hotel for a to-go breakfast.

**Warning:** Avoid scam or "impromptu guides". While you walk around temples, especially at Angkor Wat Temple, friendly Cambodians may approach you and then just start telling you interesting things about whatever you are looking at. Suddenly they will demand payment and claim you just hired them as a guide. If someone starts telling you stuff, firmly but politely say no you do not want a guide. Also, official guides have official off white shirts on, with ID cards. The others are locals taking a chance.

**Tip:** Get a 15 minute foot massage in town after each day's walking to relax your sore feet and legs so you are ready for the next day. Normally around $1.

### Get The Longer Pass

If you don't know how long you will be in Siem Reap, get the 7 day pass. For only $10 more than the 3 day pass, it is a bargain if you stay longer.

## *Tips To Take Better Pictures*

Following are some general and specific tips to help you take better pictures with from cellphones to DSLRs.

**Info:** If you want a to take just a few snapshots of the sunrise once the sun has illuminated the sky or as it peaks above the Angkor Wat towers, then a cellphone or point-and-shoot camera will work fine. If you want to get amazing pictures of the sunrise from start to finish you are going to need something better, like a DSLR or more expensive point and shoot. Normally small cameras and cellphones are only able to get good images from around 6am, when the sun isn't quite up but is lighting up the sky. By this time, you would have been standing around an hour with amazing views and unable to capture it.

### General Photo Tips

- **Practice Beforehand**. Take sunrises and sunsets with your camera or cellphone before you go to Angkor. Even at your home will help you see the limitations of your gear.
- **Go The Day Before.** It is dark when you get there in the morning, and not having any idea of how to get to the pools or where to stand can ruin your chances at a good photo. Scope it out the day or evening before.
- **Do Two Sunrises**. If it is important to you to get a good photo, go one morning and take the best pictures you can, then plan for the next day. You can then change positions, lenses or cameras the next day.
- **Focus All Around.** On small camera and cellphones, focus all around the temple and sun to get different lighting exposures (how bright the image is). Don't just point and shoot, play around a bit to change the exposure.

- **Lock Your Elbows.** If you don't have a tripod, hold you camera or phone with both hands, then lock your elbows to your sides. Set your feet apart to get a good stance. Focus the images, then take a normal breath, hold it then gently press the shutter button. You can also sit or squad down.

- **Review Your Images.** Always check your images after shooting and zoom in on the display to max to see if the shot was in focus. When dark, some camera cannot focus. Point the camera to a light spot where it can focus, hold the shutter button half in, then align the shot as you want and fully press the shutter button.

- **Shoot Raw or High Quality.** Set your Camera or cellphone to take pictures at the highest quality setting. Raw is preferred. On iPhone set to HDR.

- **Don't Kill People.** If you take pictures of someone, check that you are not cutting off parts of their heads, arms, or feet. If it is a half image, zoom in till midriff. If it is a close up, the eyes are the most important to get in and focused.

- **Charge UP!!!.** Charge your batteries the night before and bring spare batteries or an external charger for your phone. Taking pictures on cellphones eats the battery.

- **Best Times.** The best times to get good shadows and images at temples are before 10am and after 4pm.

- **Sun Behind.** Apart from sunrise and sunset, try to take pictures with the sun behind or to the side of you so that your subject is lid and you don't get a washed out sky.

- **Use People.** To add scale to how big the temples or trees are, take a picture with someone in the photo.

## Tips For Cameras

- **Take A Tripod Or Monopod.** Avoid camera shake with a steady base. A monopod is suggested as it is easier to set up, and in most cases there is just not the space to set up a tripod. Angkor can get crowded and people will bump your tripod.
- **Use A Low ISO Setting.** If you have an option on your camera, select an ISO of around 100 or so.
- **Use A UV Filter.** You may lose a bit of light, but it will help cut the glare.
- **Bracket.** Take a number of pictures while bracketing the exposure (over and under exposing the image).
- **Use Aperture Priority Mode.** If you are starting out, lock your lens aperture to make it easier. Set the lens to its widest setting early in the morning (F3.5 to 8). As more detail of the temple becomes visible, you can up the aperture to 11 or 16. The camera will then control shutter speed for you.
- **Use a Remote Trigger.** To help with vibration, use a remote trigger. If you do not have one, set your camera to 2 or 10 second timer delay.
- **More Than One Lens.** To get the best images, you are going to need more than one lens. At least an 18-24mm wide is needed for sunrise and sunset with a 12-24mm suggested. For details close up in the temple a mid-range zoom of 24-70mm is suggested. A 70-200mm (300) is suggested to isolate distant details in temples. Inside the temple, you will use 35mm a lot for shooting sections of intricate carvings, lintels and bas reliefs.

**Warning:** Don't buy a rubbish $30 knockoff tripod in Cambodia. Some fall apart and drop your camera. Either bring your own or rather use a monopod.

**Warning:** Beware of dust. Do not change lenses while riding in the tuk-tuk. Blow the dust away with an air pump at night in your hotel and use microfiber cloths, plus wet clean your sensor if needed. *Also clean your cellphone lens as it may have picked up lint or grime from staying in your pants pocket or handbag.*

**Tip:** Beware of condensation if you use an air conditioned car. You may experience condensation on your lens when you exit the cold car and walk through the hot, humid air. Do not change lenses until the camera warms up as condensation may form on your sensors. Fit the correct lens in the car beforehand.

**Tip:** Get an app on your android or IPhone that is specific for sunset and sunrise to override your camera's standard settings. There are a number of free and paid ones on the market. Try Slow Shutter Cam or NightCap Camera Pro.

## *Additional Sunrise and Sunset Locations*

There are a number of other less crowded locations you can enjoy sunrise and sunset at. Each gives you a different perspective. I suggest you do them all if you can. Sunset Time: Winter: 5:30, Spring or Fall: 6:00, Summer: 6:30. Note you can view sunset without a ticket. The park is open after 5pm.

- **Phnom Bakheng Temple.** The temple is the second most popular sunrise spot. Being high on the hill, you will have a spectacular view of the main temples of Angkor and the sun coming up behind it. Here you can get a picture of Angkor surrounded by trees and the early morning haze. <u>The temple is the spot for sunsets</u>. Go early (4pm or earlier) to ensure you get a placing as only 300 people are allowed up for sunset.
- **Srah Srang Lake.** For breath-taking sunrise views with reflecting pools head to Srah Srang. The trees surrounding the lake give spectacular reflections. Sunrise (from the embarkation terrace across Banteay Kdei) and sunset (from the East side of the Srah, closest to Pre Rup) with a reflection of the sun on the waters can be seen from here.
- **Bayon Temple.** With the stone faces, both sunset and sunrise can be enjoyed from here. Sunset however with the last rays on the faces is best here.
- **Pre Rup Temple.** The temple has three tiers. From the top level you will get a good view over the rice fields of the Eastern Baray. The brick and laterite stones give warm tones at sunset, but is good for sunrises as well.
- **Back Of Angkor Wat Temple.** At sunset from the back of Angkor Wat temple you get almost the same view as the sunrise from the front. Many do sunset at Angkor Wat Temple in front as well to get the last rays over the temple.

- **Royal Pools.** Although not as spectacular as the others, getting a reflections in the royal pools at sunrise can be good. See my picture later in the book. The bonus is that there will be almost no one there at that time.
- **Baphuon.** With its open top, Baphuon temple is a good option for both sunrise and sunset with few people around. It can be a good spot to share a romantic kiss.
- **Angkor Thom Moat.** Good for awesome sunset reflections. The best spot is from the South Gate of Angkor Thom. You will get the reflection of the sun and Angkor Thom statues.
- **Angkor Wat Moat.** Go to the east side of Angkor Wat for a beautiful sunset with the sun setting behind Angkor Wat. The trees make spectacular reflections in the moat. From the road leading from town to Angkor, turn right at the T-junction in front of Angkor Wat. Turn the corner and you'll be in position for sunset.
- **Phnom Krom**. Prasat Phnom Krom (the downstream mountain) sits on a 137m high mountain, 12.4 km from Siem Reap, on the road that leads to Tonle Sap Lake. Sunset at Phnom Krom will reward you with a view of the sun setting over Tonle Sap Lake.
- **Neak Prean.** Sunset in the wet season can be spectacular from the walkway as you are surrounded by water.
- **Preah Kahn.** Sunrise at Preah Kahn can be spectacular with the warm morning light on the eastern entrance illuminating the facade.

**Tip:** Phnom Bakheng is open till 7pm. Don't listen to anyone who tries to tell you that you're too late and won't be allowed into the temple. You also don't need to be in the temple, you can see the sunset from outside. Pre Rup is also open until 7pm.

## Temple Code of Conduct

- **No Revealing Clothes**. Cover your shoulders and knees.
- **No smoking.** Smoking is not allowed in the temples and there are no ashtrays or dustbins around the compound to dispose of your cigarette butts.
- **No Loud Noises.** Playing music, yelling or acting loudly is not allowed. You may be removed from the complex.
- **No Head Coverings.** You have to remove all head covering when entering temples. Especially the inner parts.
- **No Drones.** Drones are now banned.
- **No Giving Food, Money Or Candy To Children. Do not give money or candy to children.** Often, parents force them into the streets to work, this is child slavery.
- **No Touching Monks.** You are not allowed to touch a monk, especially women. Not even his mother may.
- **No Taking Pictures Of Monks.** Unless you asked their permission, do not take pictures of monks. Do give a small donation after taking a picture, and a proper greeting (Sampeah). Press your palms together near your heart or higher and slightly bow your head.
- **Do Give a Donation.** If you take a blessing (arm band) or incense from a monk, you are expected to give a small donation.
- **No Climbing**. Do not climb on temple walls or other parts that are not part of the official tour path.
- **No Touching.** Do not touch sculptures, shrines, bas reliefs, or other carvings. The oil and salt in your sweat over time destroys the items. Also keep your feet off the walls when you take a break and do not lean against temple pillars.
- **No Vandalism.** Do not damage any part of the temples or take any part as a keepsake. It is illegal (international art smuggling plus damaging state property). Say hello to jail.

- **No Littering.** There are a few trashcans around, but not many. Take a plastic bag with to keep your banana peels and other trash in until you get to a place to throw it away responsibly.
- **No Eating.** The temples are holy to Cambodia. Respect the culture. Eating is not allowed in the temples. Drinking water is okay.
- **Taking Commercial Film or Pictures.** If you will be using your pictures commercially, or want to film even a YouTube video, you need a permit. Large DSLR cameras, big zoom lenses, tripods, camera grab handles, large flashes, microphones, and anything that looks professional will attract attention.
- **No Naked Pictures.** That this even made the list is shocking. Unfortunately, many foreigners land up in court and jail for taking raunchy pictures. Even pulling your pants down for a bum shot is illegal. It is a holy site, think of it as going to see the Pope. If caught, you will be prosecuted and deported. If you posted the pictures online, you will also be charged with distributing pornography. They do check Facebook. You may just find that you have an international criminal record after your stunt and may be denied visas to major countries. You will also be banned from Cambodia for about 4 years or more.
- **No Poking Eyes Out.** Be careful with your umbrella and selfie stick, as well as those of others. At times the main temples can get crowded in the narrow walkways, and selfie sticks can be bumped out of your hand. Umbrellas can poke someone else in the eye in open areas of the temples that are popular.
- **No Playing With Kids.** Child abduction and pedophilia is a problem in Cambodia. Do not pick local children up, hug them or let them sit on your lap. You may attract the attention of police.

## *Tours For Disabled People*

If you are in a wheelchair or are disabled and need a wheelchair to cover large distances, take heart as you can still see Angkor Wat Temple. In fact, with a little help, there is no part of Angkor Wat Temple or any other temple that you cannot explore. If any person says you cannot see a temple, drive over their toes with your wheelchair on your way to that temple.

Most parts of all the temples, including Angkor Wat is accessible with a wheelchair if you have someone to help you over some of the entrances. Here it would be advisable to hire a local guide as they will know shortcuts to get in and can ask other locals to help them. To get to the top of Angkor Wat Temple you will need to go up around 2 flights of steep stairs. It is possible if someone can carry you up and then the wheelchair. Or as in most cases, get a few guys that carry you and your wheelchair up. At this moment there is not a lift (elevator) to take you up.

Temples such as the bottom parts of Angkor Wat Temple (**if you come from the back entrance)**, Pre Rup, Bayon, the Terrace of the Elephants & Terrace of the Leper King, some of Ta Prohm, and Banteay Srei can be done without much hassles.

I suggest a sturdy but light weight fold up wheelchair. I have no affiliation and have not use them, but you can try **http://www.angkortourguides.com/contact-us.html** as they do provide disabled tours to Angkor with specialized transport. The Lotus Lodge hotel in Siem Reap is said to be one of the best accessible for wheel chairs as the owner, Mitch St.Pierre is in a wheelchair himself. You can also try **http://www.angkortransportservice.com/package-box3.php** for transport. And read **http://travability.travel/blog-node/angkor-wat-wheelchair** (read an article by Mitch St.Pierre).

## *Vegetarian / Vegan*

Know that traditional Cambodian food is often spiced with Prahok. This gives the food a salty, pungent taste, and is a paste that is made from fermented fish (usually of mud fish). This is even put into vegetarian dishes, and in almost all soups. The Prahok shows as oily drops. Not just that it is fish (if you are vegetarian/vegan or allergic to fish), Prahok needs to be cooked or fried properly, and if not can make you very ill. Know that raw Prahok cannot be stored long, and in smaller villages it may have been cooked some time ago to preserve it.

If Prahok is not used, shrimp paste (made from fermented ground shrimp mixed with salt) is often, and is often an ingredient in dip for fish or vegetables. (This may be a bigger problem for people allergic to shellfish). Almost all fried rice are either fried in the same oil that meat was fried in, or are mixed together with egg. Go with boiled rice.

Note that most Cambodians don't know what vegetarian and vegan means. If you say no animal products, they assume beef. Thus fish, chicken, cheese, eggs and so on would be fine to them. Also, since syrup needs to be imported, most breakfast cereals are sweetened with honey as it is often locally made. Vegan cheese and meat substitutes are rare. Boiled rice, fruits and vegetables are your friends in Cambodia.

## How Safe Is Cambodia and The Temples?

Cambodia as a whole is very safe. Some parts like the beaches of Sihanoukville you do not want to walk alone at night. But Siem Reap is safe and the temples even more so. There are special tourist police patrolling the temples. A single female should have no problems exploring the temples by her own and hiring tuk-tuk drivers to take her back to the hotel.

Bag and camera snatching does happen. However rare in Siem Reap. Phnom Penh and especially Sihanoukville can be a problem. Put your bag on your lap and hold onto it while in the tuk-tuk. Put it between you and the rider if you are on a motorcycle taxi. If it is large, put it on the floor of the tuk-tuk with the straps around your legs. Don't bring any expensive jewelry to Cambodia. And don't leave any electronics in your hotel. Never leave anything laying on your bed, even if you are going to the shower or to the toilet unless all windows and doors are closed and locked. It sounds paranoid, but they do use long bamboo sticks with hooks and pull your wallet and other stuff through the window.

## What's The Weather Like?

**Cool, Rainy Season**, October to end November: Up to 30 degrees C in the daytime.
**Cool Season**, December to mid-March. Good time to visit.
**Hot Season**, mid-March to end June. In the low 40 degrees C.
**Hot, Rainy Season**, end June to September, although by end July, it is far cooler.

**Tip:** In the rainy season get a cheap emergency poncho for around 50c from any of the street sellers and keep it in your bag.

## *Angkor Kings*

Following are a short introduction to the Angkor Kings during the Angkor Empire that span from 802 to 1432. Below their names in bold is the list of any know temples they either built or made alterations to.

### Jayavarman II 802 ~ 835
*Rong Chen Temple (Phnom Kulen), early structure at Kutisvara.*
Jayavarman II is considered the founder of the Angkor Empire. He was born in 770 AD and died in 850 AD. He proclaimed himself a God King or devaraja (deva = god, raja = king) at the Kulen Mountains. To this day this magnificent waterfall where he took on the powers of the Hindu god Shiva, is sacred. If you want to visit the sacred waterfall, Kulen mountain range, Rong Chen Temple ruins, and Kbal Spean, see **https://amzn.to/2CXnhi2**

### Jayavarman III 835 ~ 877
*Prei Monti, Trapeang Phong, Bakong Temple.*
Jayavarman III was the son of Jayavarman II and the second ruler of Angkor. An inscription at Prasat Sak tells about his failed hunting experiences in trying to capture a wild elephant. He died: 877 AD, maybe from trying to capture an elephant.

### Indravarman I 877 ~ 889
*Preah Ko (at the Rolous Group), Sandstone additions to Bakong, Indratataka Baray (Baray at Roluos group that Prasat Lolei is situated in).*
Indravarman I was a usurper king. He was the nephew of Jayavarman II, and married Indradevi. He is credited for building the first baray (water reservoir). Indravarman I made the Roluos group (originally Hariharalaya) his first capital. To visit the Rolous Group temples, see Bakong Temple later in this guide.

## Yasovarman I 889 ~ 910
*Prasat Lolei, Phnom Bakheng, Prasat Bei, Thma Bay Kaek, early structure at Phimeanakas, Phnom Krom, Phnom Bok, East Baray reservoir (7 km by 1.8 km).*

Yasovarman I was Indravarman I's son. He took the sister of Jayavarman IV as his wife. He moved the capital from the Rolous Group (formerly Hariharalaya) to the Angkor (Yashodharapura) area as we know it now. He was also known as the "Leper King". Phnom Bakheng Temple was the state temple of the first capital at Angkor. An inscriptions at Banteay Chmar temple document that Yasovarman I led a failed invasion into Champa (Vietnam).

## Harshavarman I around 910 ~ around 923
*Baksei Chamkrong (at the foot of Phnom Bakheng, just before the south gate), Prasat Kravan.*

Harshavarman I was the son of Yasovarman I. His wife was Kambujarajalakshmi. During his and his younger brother's reign, there was instability in the Khmer Empire. He and his brother had to fight off their maternal uncle, Jayavarman IV who wanted the throne. He dedicated Baksei Chamrong to his parents. Prasat Kravan is said to have been built by his high-ranking priest.

## Isanavarman II 923 ~ 928
*Completed Prasat Kravan.*

Isanavarman II was the younger brother Harshavarman I. All that is know is that his reign was very chaotic. It is though that the temple Prasat Kravan was completed under his rule. Upon his death, he received a posthumous name of Paramarudraloka.

## Jayavarman IV unofficially 921, officially 928 ~ 940/1
*Koh Ker temple site.*

Jayavarman IV was another usurper. He was the brother-in-law of Jasovarman I. He was in constant power struggle with Harshavarman I and his younger brother Isanavarman II.

*Anton Swanepoel*

During the reign of Ishanavarman II, Jayavarman was driven out of Angkor and set up his own capital at Koh Ker. He succeeded as king on Isanavarman II's death. As he had his own capital, he moved the Khmer capital from Angkor to Koh Ker. The Koh Ker site was a magnificent capital and featured the largest pyramid styled temple in Cambodia. Today, around 20 structures remain in good condition. For more details, see **https://amzn.to/2IqU6DV**.

## Harshavarman II c.941/2 ~ 944
*Additional temples at Koh Ker.*
Hashavarman II was the son of Jayavarman IV. He continued construction for 3 years at Koh Ker after his father's death, then moved the capital back to Angkor (debated, see below).

## Rajendravarman II 944 ~ 968
*Pre Rup, East Mebon, Bat Chum, Kutisvara, Banteay Srei. Earlier temple on the site of Banteay Kdei, Srah Srang, Baksei Chamkrong.*
Rajendravarman II was the uncle and first cousin of Harshavarman II and son-in-law of Jayavarman IV. He took power away from Hashavarman II. There is debate as to if it was Rajendravarman II or Hashavarman II who moved the capital back to Angkor. There is also a debate about the Phimeanakas temple as some say it is Rajendravarman II and others Suryavarman I that constructed it. Like the West Mebon in the west baray, the East Mebon was built in a bary (east baray). At the time it was surrounded by water, and was a temple island. Today it is on dry land. See details later in the book. West Mebon is still surrounded by water to this day. It should be noted that Bantey Srei was built by Yajnavarah (counselor to Rajendravarman II and Jayavarman V).

### Jayavarman V 968 ~ 1001
*Ta Keo and Banteay Srei (Yajnavaraha).*
Jayavarman V was Rajendravarman II's son. He succeeded his father when he was only ten years old and became the youngest king ever of Cambodia. Jayavarman V studied under Yajnavaraha, a grandson of King Harshavarman I. When he turned seventeen years old, he began the construction of Ta Keo. A thunderbolt hit the edifice during construction. This was seen as a bad omen. Priests were called to perform a ritual to dispel the demons, but it was of no success. The temple was left unfinished. Although Hindu in believe, he allowed Buddhism to flourish. He also allowed women to hold high positions in all ranks.

### Udayadityavarman I 1001 ~ 1002
Udayadityavarman I was the nephew of Jayavarman V. He succeeded the throne through violent conflict, but was killed in 1002.

### Jayaviravarman I 1002 ~ 1010
*North Khleang, additions to Ta Keo.*
Jayaviravarman I ascended the supreme throne, but Suryavarman I also proclaimed himself king and consistently challenged Jayaviravarman I. A violent power struggle ensued. In 1010, Suryavarman I managed to overthrow Jayaviravarman I.

### Suryavarman I 1002 ~ 1049
*South Khleang, Preah Vihear in the Dangrek Mountains, Phimeanakas, Royal Palace, Suryaparvata at Phnom Chisor, Preah Khan at Kompong Svay, West Baray, Wat Phu, completed Ta Keo.*
Suryavarman I unofficially proclaimed himself king in 1002 after killing Udayadityavarman I. Suryavarman I was the son of the King of Tambralinga (a Tamil-Malay state on the Malay Peninsula).

Suryavarman I claimed royal linage through his mother that was of the royal line of Indravarman I. He officially became king in 10110 after overthrowing Jayaviravarman I. He allowed Buddhism to flourish in Cambodia.

Suryavarman I promoted many public works, such as irrigation projects, constructing monasteries, and developing the Angkor area. He expanded the Khmer empire into the Mae Nam Valley west of the Tonle Sap (Great Lake), as well as vast tracts of land on the fringes of southern Laos. After ousting Jayaviravarman I, Cambodia was a land of domestic peace and prosperity. On his death in 1049, he received the posthumous title of Nirvanapada (the king, who had gone to Nirvana).

### Udayadityavarman II 1049 ~ 1066
*Baphuon, West Mebon, completed construction of West Baray.*
Udayadityavarman II was the younger nephew of Suryavarman I. His royal lineage came from Yasovarman I's spouse. During his rule Cambodia was at relative peace.

### Harshavarman III 1066 ~ 1080
Harshavarman III was the younger brother of Udayadityavarman II. He made his capital at Baphuon temple that was built by his brother. His rule was plagued by internal rebellions as well as invasion by the Champa (between 1074 and 1080). Some of the temples at Sambhupra were destroyed and many of the inhabitants were taken into slavery to My Son.

### Nripatindravarman I 1080 ~ around 1118
After the death of Harshavarman III, Cambodia was thrown into chaos and internal conflict. Records are scares and unclear. It seems that there may have been two kings trying to rule at the same time. Nripatindravarman I was thought to be the successor of Harshavarman III with those who remained loyal to the legitimate line of Harshavarman III.

He may have ruled in Cambodia while Jayavarman VI ruled from what is now known as Thailand. From records of Suryavarman II stating that he took power from two kings, it gives weight that the country was split with two rules and that Nripatindravarman I was killed or overthrown by Suryavarman II.

### Jayavarman VI 1080 ~ c.1107
*Phimai Temple.*
Jayavarman VI was another usurper king. He came from Phimai, Mun River Valley, on the Khorat Plateau, in present-day Thailand. It is suggested that he may have been a vassal prince as during the reigns of Udayadityavarman II and Harshavarman III there was war with Champa and internal rebellions. From inscriptions, he claimed to be a descendant of the mythical couple of prince Sage Kambu Swayambhuva and his sister (and wife) Mera. This gives further speculation that he had no real ancestors of royal lineage. Jayavarman VI was probably engaged for several years in strife against Nripatindravarman I.

Jayavarman VI is credited with building the Phimai temple, one of the largest Khmer temples of Thailand. The temple is located in the town of Phimai, Nakhon Ratchasima. The temple was one end of the Ancient Khmer Highway from Angkor to Thailand. The size of the temple compares to that of Angkor Wat in outer dimensions. However, it was not as high and elaborate. Phimai must have been an important city to construct and gives further weight that Jayavarman VI may have been a vassal prince. It is possible that Jayavarman VI ruled from Phimai.

### Dharanindravarman I 1107 ~ 1112/3
Dharanindravarman I was the elder brother of Jayavarman VI and took over the throne on Jayavarman VI's death. He was married to Queen Vijayendralakshmi, former wife of Jayavarman VI. Following the death of Jayavarman VI, Cambodia was thrown even more into chaos.

This was possibly due to Nripatindravarman I trying to wrestle power away from Dharanindravarman I. Dharanindravarman I was murdered in battle by his great-nephew, Suryavarman II.

### Suryavarman II 1113 (self-proclaimed), 1119 (officially) ~ around 1150

*Angkor Wat Temple, Thommanon, Chao Say Tevoda, Banteay Samre, Phnom Rung (in present—day Thailand), Beng Mealea.*
Suryavarman II was the younger nephew of Dharanindravarman I. He was born in Lopburi as Narith, the son of Ksitindraditya, who was brother of Dharanindravarman. Lopburi is about 150 kilometers northeast of Bangkok, in modern day Thailand.

Narith studied under a Divakarapandita (original name Divakara). Divakarapandita was a Brahman priest, born 1040, died 1120. Narith was a very skilled warrior and was said to be wise beyond his years.

Divakarapandita who served king Harshavarman II, Jayavarman VI, and Dharanindravarman I, took notice of Narith. With the old king Dharanindravarman I unable to effectively rule the country, Divakarapandita and a number of other priests backed Narith as ruler for Cambodia. When king Dharanindravarman I traveled through Narith's district, he was ambushed and killed. An inscription reads "Bounding on the head of the elephant of the enemy king, he killed him, as Garuda on the edge of a mountain would kill a serpent." Garuda, in Hindu mythology is a kite or an eagle and the vahana (mount) of the god Vishnu. It should be noted that scholars do not agree on if this inscription refers to him killing king Dharanindravarman I or Nripatindravarman. However, another inscription does collaborate that Narith killed king Dharanindravarman I. Narith was crowned king by Divakarapandita in 1113 and took on the name Suryavarman II (Shield of the Sun).

He was said to be 17 at the time. However, as he was from a line of kings that was contested by the people of the south, he had to embark on a military campaign to establish total rule. This was possibly against king Nripatindravarman I, who was thought to have been the successor of king Harshavarman III. It is thought to have taken 6 years before Suryavarman II crushed all opposition. He was official crowed king of Cambodia in 1119 at the royal palace of Angkor, at the age of 23. Divakarapaṇḍita again oversaw the ceremony and crowned him king.

Suryavarman II made his soldiers and subjects swore and oath of loyalty to him. Translated into English it reads. "We will serve no other king. We will sacrifice our lives in the face of war. We will be reborn in the 32 levels of hell if we break our oath."

Having met Princess Suryavana Devi of Champa before becoming king, he married her and took her as his only wife. In fact, Suryavarman II was one of a few kings that had only one wife and no consorts, (many other kings has up to 5 wives and 3000 consorts). He had one child and was the second youngest king to rule Cambodia. Suryavarman II was skilled in war tactics, knew Sanskrit and Khmer culture. He reunited the empire and vastly expanded the Khmer territory to include much of what is now Thailand. His patronage stretched as far west as the frontiers of the Burmese state of Pagan, south to the coast of the Gulf of Thailand, part of the eastern coast of the Malay Peninsula, and east to the kingdom of Champa (modern Vietnam).

Since Suryavarman II was an unsurper king, he had to prove he was selected by the gods to rule. From advice from Divakarapaṇḍita, he started construction of Angkor Wat. It is thought that construction only started in 1120.

In 1116 Suryavarman II resumed diplomatic relations with the Chinese. In 1128 China officially recognized his kingdom as their vassal. By sending tributes to China, he gained a powerful ally. From 1123 until 1138 Suryavarman II waged a number of unsuccessful campaigns against Dai Viet, the Vietnamese kingdom. In 1128 he attempted a land attack though Laos to Nghe An and met with defeat. In 1129 he used the Mekong River and took 700 ships with 20K soldiers to harass Champa along the coast in the Gulf of Tonkin. In 1132 and 1138 he again failed to invade Champa. Finally in 1144 Suryavarman II won and deposed of the Cham king. He annexed Champa in 1145 and sacked the capital Vijaya. Suryavarman II made his brother-in-law, Harideva, king of Cham. However, the Chams chose their own ruler, king Jaya Harivarman I. Under his rule they defeated the Khmer troops at Chakling, near Phan Rang, in southern Vietnam.

Jaya Harivarman I deposed of Harideva and reclaimed the Champa territory. In a revenge attack to dispose of Jaya Harivarman I, Suryavarman II died. As the campaign started in 1145, it is not clear when exactly Suryavarman II died. It is believed he died between 1145 and 1150. It is also not know if he died in battle or after battle from wounds he sustained. He can be seen on many of the bas reliefs at Angkor Wat, and is the only king to be featured on bas reliefs at Angkor. After his death he was given the name, Paramavishnuloka: "He who lives with Vishnu." This new name is on a bas relief at Angkor Wat Temple. This gives weight that Suryavarman II may have been buried at the temple after his death, even though the temple was not complete at the time.

### Dharanindravarman II around 1150 ~ 1160
Dharanindravarman II was the younger nephew of Jayavarman VI. He was the son of the brother of Suryavarman II's mother (Narendralakshmi). He had married Princess Sri Jayarajacudamani, the daughter of Harshavarman III.

In 1120 they had a son called Jayavarman VII that would become king later. During Dharanindravarman II's reign Cambodia was in constant turmoil with internal conflict and attacks from Vietnam.

### Yasovarman II around 1160 ~ 1165
*Beng Mealea, Chao Say Tevoda, Banteay Samre, Bakong.*
Yasovarman II was the parent of Dharanindravarman II. He took over from Dharanindravarman II for unknown reasons. In 1165 he was assassinated by one of his own subordinates.

### Tribhuvanadityavarman 1165 ~ 1177
Tribhuvanadityavarman was a mandarin and usurper king. Although many subjects still supported Yasovarman II's linage, he managed to hold the throne against them and quell all uprisings. However, he had to content with attacks from Champa. King Jaya Indravarman III from Champa invaded and sacked Angkor. However, Tribhuvanadityavarman managed to kill Jaya Indravarman III. In 1177 king Jaya Indravarman IV from Champa travelled up the Mekong and Tonle Sap rivers to Tonle Sap Lake and successfully invaded Angkor, and killed Tribhuvanadityavarman.

### Cham Occupation 1177 ~ 1178
During this time Cambodia was occupied by Cham (Vietnam) forces and was under their rule. The king at the time was Jaya Indravarman IV (1167–1192).

### Jayavarman VII 1181 ~ around 1218
*Ta Prohm, Preah Khan, Jayatataka baray (baray Neak Pean is in), Neak Pean, Ta Som, Ta Nei, Banteay Chhmar, Angkor Thom, the four Prasat Chrungs (structures in the four corners of Angkor Thom City) Bayon, Elephant Terrace, Ta Prohm Kel, Hospital Chapel, Krol Ko, Srah Srang, Royal Palace.*

Jayavarman VII was the son of Dharanindravarman II. He married Princess Jayarajadevi. After her death, he married her sister Indradevi. It is though that both his wives where the influence behind his Buddhist devotion. He was the second Buddhist king. He is considered to have been the most powerful of the Khmer monarchs. He built Bayon temple as a Buddhist shrine.

In 1178, Jayavarman VII led a Khmer army against the Cham occupation. This conflict included a naval battle that is depicted on the walls of Bayon and Banteay Chmar temples. Jayavarman VII successfully ousted the invaders, then turned his attention to the divided Cambodian factions. In 1181 after having defeated opposing royals, he crowned himself king. He expanded Khmer control of the Mekong Valley northward to Vientiane and to the south, down the Kra Isthmus. Jayavarman VII embarked on many public works and cared greatly for his people. He is credited for the construction of 102 hospitals, rest houses along the roads, and reservoirs. He built Ta Prohm in honor of his mother and Preah Khan in honor of his father.

### Indravarman II around 1218 ~ 1243
*Prasats Suor Prat, Ta Prohm, Banteay Kdei, Ta Som, Ta Nei.*
Indravarman II was the son of Jayavarman VII. There is some disagreement to when he actually ruled as there is only one mention of him on an inscription, and that says that he died 1143. He followed the Buddhist tradition. During his reign, Cambodia was mostly peaceful. The kingdom did however lose control of Champa.

### Jayavarman VIII c.1243 ~ 1295
*Mangalartha, Preah Palilay (debated), Bayon, Ta Prohm, Preah Khan, Prasat Chrungs (structures in the four corners of Angkor Thom City), Angkor Wat, Baphuon, Chao Say Tevoda, Banteay Samre, Beng Mealea, Terrace of the Leper King, Elephant Terrace, Preah Pithu, Royal Palace.*

Jayavarman VIII was the son of Indravarman II. He reverted back to Hinduism and made it the state religion. In 1281, Jayavarman VIII imprisoned emissaries of the Mongol generalissimo in Champa. In 1283, the Mongols under the command of Kublai Khan attacked Angkor. Jayavarman VIII made peace with the Mongols by paying tributes. However, he was locked in a devastating war with the Sukhothai Kingdom that was an early kingdom in north central Thailand. In 1295, he was overthrown by his son-in-law Indravarman III (Srindravarman).

### Srindravarman (Indravarman III) 1295 ~ 1307
*Ta Prohm, Preah Pithu, Preah Palilay.*
Srindravarman was the son-in-law of Jayavarman VIII. He married Srindrabhupesvarachuda, the eldest daughter of Jayavarman VIII. Having a line to the throne, he overthrew his father in law and reinstated Buddhism as the state religion.

### Srindrajayavarman (Indrajayavarman or Indravarman I) 1307 ~ 1327
Not much is known about about Srindrajayavarma except that he turned the state religion back to Hinduism.

### Jayavarman Paramesvara (Jayavarman IX) 1327 ~ 1336
Jayavarman IX was the son of Indrajayavarman. He was accidentally killed in 1336 by the head of the royal gardens, Neay Trasac Paem Chay.

### Neay Trasac Paem Chay 1336 ~ 1340
Neay Trasac Paem Chay is thought to have accidentally killed Jayavarman Paramesvara. He then married the daughter of Jayavarman Paramesvara and took the throne. He is the first Khmer ruler mentioned only by the Royal Chronicles of Cambodia.

There is a legend that states that he was the son of a Phnom Kulen hermit and a Samre peasant. He was a cucumber farmer and grew such sweet cucumbers that the king gave him a spear to protect the cucumbers. Only the king was allowed to eat the cucumbers. One night the king went into the gardens to get cucumbers. Not realizing it is the king, Neay Trasac Paem Chay wounded the king. The king forgave him and said that he only followed orders to protect the cucumbers. In a ceremony to elect a new king as the old one had no sons, Chay was elected king by the people of the village. It is said that he moved the capital from Angkor to Banteay Samre.

### Nippean Bat 1340 ~1346
Nippean Bat (Nirvana Pada) was the eldest son of Neay Trasac Paem Chay. Like his father, he is only mentioned in the Royal Chronicles. During his reign Cambodia lost all their hold on the Thai dependent states.

### Sithean Reachea 1346 ~ 1347
Sithean Reachea was the second and younger son of Neay Trasac Paem Chay. According to the Royal Chronicles he only ruled for around 3 to 6 months before giving the throne over to his nephew Lampong Reachea.

### Lampong Reachea (Parama Radjadiraja) 1347 ~ 1351
Lampong Reachea was the nephew of Sithean Reachea. Under his rule, war with the former Thais vassal erupted. In 1351 the Thais managed to march right to the walls of Angkor where they were halted and pushed back. However, King Ramathibodi from Thailand invested more troops to the attack and besiege Angkor for a year. The siege generated famine and sickness. In this time King Lampong Reachea died of illness. Angkor was sacked and looted. The Khmer treasures and court dancers were taken to Thailand. From 1352 to 1357 Cambodia was under Thai rule.

**Soryavong (Soriyotei or Surya-vamça Radhadiraja) 1357 ~ 1366**
Soriyotei (also known as Sri Suriya Daya) was a younger brother of King Lampong Reachea and second son of King Nippean Bat. He had escaped from Angkor before the capture of the city, and took refuge in Laos with some warriors. In 1357 he surprised the Thai invaders at Angkor with a band of Khmer irregulars. At the time Siamese king Chau Combang Pissey ruled. Soryavong ousted the king and took over power. He managed to repel the Thais to beyond Korat and Prachinburi and restored the border with Champa. He died of illness in around 1366.

### Barom Reamea 1366 ~ 1373

Barom Reamea was the nephew of Soryavong and son of Lampong Reachea. Cambodia endured a time of piece under his reign. He made contact with Hong-Wu, the first emperor of the Ming Dynasty and developed trade relations.

### Thommo Soccoroch 1373 ~ 1394

Thommo Soccoroch (Dhammasoka Reachea) was the youngest son of Lampong Reachea and brother to Barom Reamea. During his reign he intensified relations with the Chinese Ming dynasty. In 1394 Thailand attacked and besieged Angkor for seven months. Due to the betrayals of a Khmer princes, Angkor was sacked. King Thommo Soccoroch was killed and around 70,000 prisoners were deported to Thailand as slaves. King Ramesuan of Thailand appointed his son Ento as king of Cambodia.

### Soriyovong 1401 ~ 1417

In 1401, Khmer prince Soriyovong, son of the former king Soriyotei I, managed to assassinate Ento and reclaim the throne.

### Barom Soccoroch 1417 ~ 1421

Barom Soccoroch is thought to be either the son of King Thommo Soccarach or Dhammasoka Reachea I or the nephew of King Soriyovong. His reign ended when Thais one again sacked Angkor.

### Ponhea Yat Chao 1421 ~ 1467

Ponhea Yat Chao was the son of Soriyovong and cousin of Barom Soccoroch. He was the last king of the Angor Era. Ponhea Yat moved the capital to Angkor Thom. He was ousted as king in 1431 when Thai armies destroyed the Khmer capital. In 1432 he abandoned Angkor and moved the capital to Chaktomuk (modern day Phnom Penh). In 1445 he managed to expel the Thai usurper king at Angkor but kept the capital at Chaktomuk.

## *Angkor Wat*

**Date:** Thought to be 1120 ~ around 1152.
**King:** Suryavarman II (shield of the sun).
**Religion:** Hindu.
**Style:** Angkor Wat.
**Time:** Minimum 1 day, (suggests two half days, morning and afternoon).
**Importance:** The largest religious monument in the world. Longest complete bas-relief in the world.
**My Impression:** I was blown away by the size of the temple complex. Even after visiting the complex over 30 times, it still leaves an impression on me. When you walk over the baray between all the other people, you first think that it is going to be a shoulder-to-shoulder visit.

However, once inside the temple grounds, the complex just swallows the people up to the point, you wonder if you did not get the memo to evacuate. The climb to the top of the central sanctuary is steep, but the 360-degree view provided by a number of open windows on the large top area, is well worth it.

**Best Time To Visit:** Early in the morning to catch the sun rising over Angkor, and late afternoon to get good pictures of the sun from behind you. To avoid the crowds, come at midday when everyone else is eating.

**GPS:** 13°24'45.2"N 103°51'34.1"E.

Angkor Wat ([city] [temple or pagoda]) is 1.6km (1 mile) from the south gate of Angkor Thom City (main entrance), and is the most impressive temple in the Angkor Wat Archaeological Park. The park itself is roughly the size of Manhattan in New York. Although temples in the park date from the 9th to the 14th century, Angkor Wat Temple was constructed during the first half of the 12th century (around 1120 to 1152), by King Suryavarman II. The base of the temple is 330m long x 255m wide (1089 ft. long x 841 ft. wide). An outer wall spanning an impressive 1.5km (0.93 miles) long x 1.3 km (0.8 miles) wide, surrounds the temple complex. The complex can cover the flight decks of more than 100 aircraft carriers.

This outer wall is further surrounded by a 190m (623 feet) wide moat (size of channel from shore to shore). The main entrance to the temple grounds is on the western end by means of a 12m (39 feet) wide x 190m (623 feet) long bridge that crosses the moat. Lions and Naga snakes guard the start of the bridge. The temple has many smaller library buildings that surround it, as well as an inner and outer courtyard. The central temple has multiple levels, with five large towers on the top level.

The central shrine on the top level is 65 meter high, as tall as the Notre-Dame Cathedral in Paris. Indian mythology dominates Angkor Wat Temple due to trade with India. The monsoon winds blew the Indian trader's ships from India to Asia where they mingled with local Khmer people for around six months while they waited for the trade winds to reverse direction. During this annual six months mingle, a lot of Indian believes and traditions were integrated into the Khmer culture.

Angkor Wat Temple is believed to represent Mount Meru, the center of the world in Hindu cosmology and the Indian home of the gods and is believed to be a mythical place somewhere north of the Himalayas. The temple's five sanctuary towers represent the peaks of the sacred mountain, while the moat around the temple represents the ocean that surrounds Mount Meru. The towers imitate the shape of a closed lotus blossom.

Intricate bas-reliefs spanning almost 600 meters (2600 feet) depict scenes from epic Ramayana and Mahabharata battles and events from Khmer history. Most of these bas-reliefs were covered in a thin layer of gold with a red background. The most famous and arguably the most fascinating bas-relief is of the turning of the sea of milk, where the gods and demons worked together to generate the elixir of live. There are also 1796 apsara dancers carved into stone all around Angkor Wat. They represent the earthly version of the cosmic apsaras or nymphs. Each one is unique in looks, style and dress. They are thought to have been modelled from actual court dancers at the temple.

The temple is unlike other Angkor temples in orientation, facing west and dedicated to Vishnu, where other temples face east and are dedicated to Shiva. Some believe the west facing was that the temple served as a funerary temple, as the setting sun symbolizes the end of the cycle of life. Some evidence to back this up was found in the temple.

Surprisingly, Angkor Wat Temple itself was not built to pray in. It was the home of Vishnu and his lesser gods. All the corridors are space for the minor gods of India that come with the main god. The steps that one now take to the top shrine, were once barred to only the holiest of priests who were the caretakers of the place as well as the God. The king prayed here to Vishnu. The priests anointed and clothed the statues inside Angkor Wat. The main shrine on the top is smaller than most people's living room, yet even today is seen as extremely holy.

The libraries around the temple ground were once filled with ancient manuscripts made from palm leaves. These holy books were the greatest treasures the Buddhist monasteries had and were used to teach new monks. Angkor Wat also contains numerous carved Sanskrit inscriptions, giving a record of Angkor Wat's past. Battles, everyday life, as well as a list of kings are recorded in the inscriptions. To date, over 1200 transcripts have been translated at Angkor Wat.

Angkor Wat Temple took around 32 years to build, and is an architectural wonder. Just clearing the area of trees with machetes and axes was an enormous task. Only Salisbury cathedral was built in the same time span as Angkor Wat. Most over cathedrals of the time took 200 to 300 years to build, and they are significantly smaller than Angkor Wat. The temple is in fact, floating on an artificial island, with the massive surrounding moat, providing water to keep the temple floating in the dry season. This ingenious setup allows the complex to be at ground level, without the need to be built on a mount as other large temples.

Temples built directly on the ground eventually crumble to pieces due to the shifting sand. In the heavy monsoon rain season, the ground expands when being water logged.

During the dry season, the ground dries and contracts again. This constant cycle of expansion and contraction eventually causes temples not build on a mount to collapse. There are 1532 columns at Angkor Wat, each weighing around 2 tons. However, the friction of the stones is not enough to keep the temple in place. Cambodians used their knowledge of woodworking and how shapes interlocked to make grooves and locks to allow the stones to interlock into each other.

Interestingly, builders did not use the common method of using a keystone arch, but rather used corbelling. With corbelling, builders placed a block, then another block on top of it, but slightly off-center. They kept on placing blocks off-center until the archway connected at the top. According to modern architects, this method should not work on the scale of Angkor Wat. Yet, Angkor Wat is the largest stone temple in the world, and still standing.

Because Angkor Wat was to be a sacred temple, it had to be built on pure ground. The sand at the building site had to be excavated down several meters. This sand would later be used as filling for the several layers of Angkor Wat temple. Walls of interlocking blocks kept the sand from sliding down. The buttresses alongside the steps leading up on each layer of Angkor Wat helps the terraces and stone walls not to give into the weight of the sand. Records in bass-reliefs at Bayon show how they build Angkor. Hundreds of thousands of workers from all over the kingdom were brought in for the project. It is estimated that it took around 5000 workers just to dig the moat around Angkor Wat. Both the inside and outside walls of the moat are lined with sandstone to keep the water in. Once the site was excavated, a thick layer of blessed sand was used to fill the site. A layer of rocks was used to top the sand layer, and a final layer of fine sand was placed over the rock layer. The fine layer of sand was compacted and leveled, and then priests came and asked the gods to bless the site and temple.

Priest dipped cords into colored powder and lay them down in patterns. The cords were then picked up and dropped, so that colored mandala patterns were made on the ground. These patterns represent heaven and symbolically the priests bound the gods to the site to ensuring the gods' blessings on the temple. Two offerings were then placed at the center of the temple. 2 White Safire stones that represent the moon, and 2 gold leaves that signify the sun. The engineers erected an 89 feet tall shaft over the buried offerings that leads thought the temple to the sacred central chamber above. The temple was erected around the shaft in layers with terraces stacked on top of one another. The second and third level is twice as high as the first. Completed, the structure weighs thousands of tons. The top of the shaft was guarded by a statue of Vishnu, which was later replaced by an image of Buddha that is said to remain to this day. It is thought to be the one holding both hands up.

The sand and silt that were removed from the moat alone are estimated to be 5 million cubic meters, around 200 000 dump trucks. This sand was used with the excavated sand for the temple to fill the terraces that are contained by stonewalls. The cliffs of the rivers of the holy Kulen Mountain 30 kilometers away were the source of the rocks used for the temple.

It is estimated that workers needed to transport around 300 to 400 blocks of stone weighing 3 to 12 tons each, per day, for 32 years. Workers used chisels to trench the stone, and then inserted wooden wedges. The wedges were then drenched with water, causing them to expand and split the stone. Holes were made in the stones so that wooden pegs could be inserted. This allowed workers to maneuver the blocks. Angkor Wat was built using laterite, a rock formation normally consisting of iron, aluminum, and quarts.

It is believed that the rocks were placed on barges, and then pulled by animals on the banks to the temple site. Animals used were possibly elephants or water buffalos. At the site, blocks were shaped by grinding them over each other. This process creates a perfect flat contact for the entire surface of the stone and is called abrasion. The laterite was covered by a layer of sandstone. The sandstone layer allowed carvers to carve the intricate bas-reliefs. In only a few millimeters of sandstone at places, multiple depths of fields were carved. Experts believe that the carvings took almost half the time of the building of the temple itself. To speed up the process, master carvers would outline the design, and then junior carvers would complete the carving by following the outline. For the bas-relief carvings, when done, it was covered in a layer of gold or paint.

The temple as you see it now was not as it was. The outer walkway pillars where thought to have been white from a lime covering. The roof lintels and inner wooden doors where gold covered. The inner pillars where red with gold trim. The 5 towers are thought to have been totally covered in gold. The roof stones may have been white or very light blue. Even the floor may have been white.

Because 88% of the year's rain falls during the monsoon season of only a few months, Angkor Wat had to have drainage systems in place. The outside of the passages have interlocking roof stones that have channels cut into them. These channels allow water to be channeled away before it seeps through the roof and floods the passages. Interestingly, although the temple was dedicated to Vishnu, the faces at Angkor Wat is that of Suryavarman II. Like the temples at Egypt, Angkor Wat had to be completed before Suryavarman II died to allow him to join the gods. There is evidence that construction was hurried on parts of the temple, and at places, not all decorations were completed. According to tradition, the king would have been cremated and his ashes placed in a stone casket in the temple.

Such a casket was found at Angkor Wat, but at the wrong place. The casket could have been moved when Champa (Vietnam) invaders sacked Angkor Wat. The invaders made off with the entire royal dance court, and they became the start of traditional Asia dancing. Interestingly, Thai fighting and much of Thai cooking also originated from Cambodia. Although the Cambodians eventually drove the invaders out and defeated them on the Tonle Sap Lake, Angkor Wat was mostly abandoned as a Royal temple.

Although others visited the temple over the years, it was brought to the world's attention in 1860 by the illustrations of French naturalist and explorer Henri Mouhot, on an expedition to Cambodia. 500 years of jungle was painstakingly removed, and damaged sections repaired. Today, Angkor Wat features on the Cambodian national flag, and is a major pull for tourists to Cambodia.

There was a legend that under Angkor Wat was a massive royal treasury. Access was thought to have been though the central shaft. In the 1930s Marchal and Georges Trouvè investigated the main shaft. For 8 months, they dug into the shaft but was hampered by monsoon rains. The shaft constantly filling up with water. They eventually managed to get pumps to the temple and drained the water. One day in 1934, just after dawn, workers came to woke Trouvè. Excitedly he followed them to the shaft. The men had dug up the stone box containing the gold leaves and Safire offerings to Vishnu. Trouvè was warned not to remove the sacred objects, but ignored it. He mysteriously died a few months later in 1935. The Safire stones and gold leaves disappeared.

After the main entrance gate, is a 350m (1148 feet) processional causeway that is elevated about 1½ meters (5 feet). This causeway is flanked by a library building on either side, followed by two pools directly in front of Angkor Wat. From here, one enters the outer courtyard that has a few shuttle buildings. The inner courtyard wall contains the bas-reliefs. Once past the inner courtyard wall, stairs give access to the main temple structure.

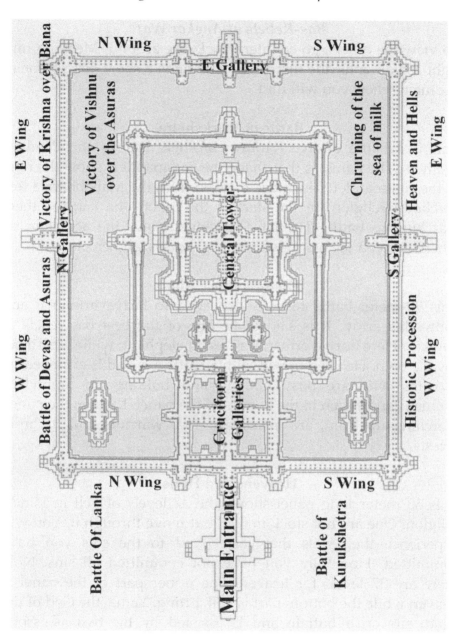

### Bas-Reliefs at Angkor Wat

To view the reliefs, go counter -clockwise around. Meaning turn right as you enter the temple. Following is a short description of the main reliefs you will find.

### Battle of Kurkshetra

This is a battle of five Kaurava brothers against the Pandava brothers. The parasols that shade the commanders show the rank of the commander. The scene is taken from the Mahabharata text in Hindu religion. In the start of the relief, you can see them marching to battle. The later carvings shows the actual battle where you can see wounded soldiers, horses, and chiefs.

### Historic Procession

This 90 meter battle relief is dedicated to Suryavarman II and shows his army. It is said to be one of the best bas reliefs at Angkor. Here Suryavarman II rides an elephant, while wearing a royal crown. He is equipped with a battle axe and is encircled by servants who are busy fanning and holding up umbrellas. Women can be seen in the bottom of the panel. Later in the panel, marching up front, are mercenary Thai warriors and Brahmin priests.

### Heavens and Hells

This 60 meter long panel shows the 32 levels of hell in Hindu religion. One are not stuck in hell, but move through it. You will experience the levels that correspond to the sins you have committed. Hopefully you have not committed all sins. Note there are 37 levels for heaven. The upper part of the panel is heaven while the bottom part is hell, fitting. Yama, the God of the dead, sits on a buffalo and is assisted by his two assessors, Dharma and Sitragupta. There are 36 short inscriptions on the panel. As expected, life in heaven depicts rich palaces, flying Apsara nymphs, and lavish draperies. Life in hell is just torture with boiling people, breaking bones, burning with hot irons, piercing heads with nails, and more. No thanks.

**The Churning of the Sea of Milk**

This is probably the most famous of all. It depicts the 92 gods pulling on the body of the giant naga (serpent) Vasuki, which is coiled around Mount Mandara. Vishnu is in the form of the tortoise. They pull for 1000 years against 88 demons and create the elixir of immortality. Fish and crocodiles were cut into pieces by the turning action. The Apsaras (heavenly nymphs) were released into the world from the cosmic world in the process. Off course, once the elixir was created, Vishnu took the elixir for himself. Legend says that one demon sneaked into Vishnu's residence and drank the elixir before Vishnu beheaded him. But due to the elixir he survived, but possessed only his head.

**Victory of Vishnu over The Asuras (Demons)**

Here Vishnu is riding a Garuda (a mythical bird) while he is slaying demons. He is surrounded by two armies, but Vishnu wreaks havoc among them and sends them running.

**Victory of Krishna over Bana (the Demon King)**

Here, Vishnu is incarnated as Krishna. He has eight arms and multiple heads. While riding a Garuda, he confronts Bana. Krishna is assisted by Agni, the god of Fire. Agni helps Krishna douse the defensive fires that surround Bana's castle. After capturing Bana, the mortal form of Vishnu (Krishna) pleads with Shiva for Bana's life at Mt. Kailasa. The goddess Parvati and the elephant god Ganesha (remover of obstacles) are also present.

**Battle of Devas (Gods) and Asuras (Demons)**

Here, 21 gods are fighting the asuras. Vishnu is on his garuda. Yama (god of the dead) is riding on a chariot that is pulled by oxen. Shiva is readying his bow. Brahma is on the sacred goose. Surya (god of sun) is standing on a sun disc. Indra is standing on his elephant with four tusks. Skanda (god of war) is perched on his peacock.

### Battle of Lanka (Ceylon /Sri Lanka)

The relief shows scenes from Ramayana in Mahabharata. Rama tries to rescue his wife Sita from Ravana (the kidnapper). Rama is standing on the shoulders of Hanuman (the monkey god), with Lakhsmana (Rama's brother) and Vibishana (a giant) behind him. Later, Ravana is standing on a war chariot that is pulled by lions. This panel is said to be one of the prettiest at Angkor Wat.

### *Angkor Wat Walkthrough*

To get to the outer wall, you have to cross over a 200-meter (656 feet) wide moat. A sandstone causeway, 250 meters long (820 feet) and 12 meters wide (39 feet), crosses the moat. The moat has a perimeter of 5.5 kilometers (3.4 miles). Including the moat, the Angkor Wat Temple compound forms a rectangle of about 1,500 by 1,300 meters, around 208 hectares (500 acres).

In December and January, the moat is full. The moat is another good place to do sunrises and sunsets. You can get the trees reflecting on the water with the temple in the background of your images.

Once you crossed the moat, you will come to the outer wall. The outer wall is 1024 meters (3,360 feet) by 802 meters (2,631 feet) and 4.5 meters (15 feet) high. It is surrounded by a 30 meter (98 feet) apron of open ground.

After the gate, is a 350-meter (1148 feet) processional causeway, elevated about 1½ meters (5 feet), flanked by a library building on either side, followed by two pools.

*350-meter (1148 feet) processional causeway.*

*One of the libraries alongside the causeway towards the temple.*

The main image at the start for Angkor Wat is from behind the left pool. This is where you want to stand to get sunrise pictures of Angkor wat. If getting the sun behind the central pillar is not all-important, go to the pool on the right. It is far less crowded.

Once you passed the libraries, you will get to the next level. This is where you enter the temple structure. To view the bas reliefs, go counter-clockwise around. There are a number of entrances to use. In the western entrance of Angkor Wat is a 5 meter (16 ½ foot), sandstone statue of Vishnu, known as Ta Reach. It is beneath a parasol. It is believed that this statue may have been the one that was first put in the top tower to guard the main shaft when Angkor Was build. It is said that when the temple was converted to Buddhism, the head was replaced with that of Buddha. The original head was restored in 2000.

The two entrances on either side of the structure is referred to as "elephant gates", as they are large enough to admit elephants. On the outer (west) side, there are square pillars, and on the inner (east) side, a closed wall. These pillars are thought to have been white due to a layer of lime. The ceiling is decorated with lotus rosettes. There is an Apsara with her mouth open and showing her teeth. She is said to be the only one in all the temples, but this is not so. There was one other found at another temple. The one at Temple is behind and to the right of the multi-armed statue of Vishnu. As you walk around the temple complex, admire the other celestial nymphs (Apsaras). There are 1796 of them at Angkor Wat.

Next picture is the pillars on the outer edge of the walkway. There are 1532 of them. They are all solid blocks and weigh around 2 tons. The walkway is 2.45 meters (8 feet) wide.

*Some of the bas-reliefs you will see.*

*Apsara showing her teeth.*

*Multi armed Vishnu (Ta Reach).*

By the main entrance, you will be close to the cruciform galleries. There are two halls and four square water basins. The water basins are thought to have been used by the king and priests to cleanse themselves before they go up to the central tower.

If you were to go either left or right and step out of the cruciform galleries you would be in the outer courtyard. There are two libraries on either side of the cruciform galleries at the edges of the courtyard. You can walk all around the temple and use any of the steps to get back to the central part. The temple platform is 330 meter long (1083 feet) x 255 meter (837 feet) wide.

If you use any of the steps from the courtyard or if you went from the cruciform galleries directly up, you would come to the inner courtyard. Here are a number of smaller structures.

*Outer courtyard.*

*Inner courtyard viewed from atop.*

Once you had your fill of the inner courtyard, head to the steps leading to the top. A 42m high central sanctuary, with Buddha statues, is situated in the middle of the Angkor Wat complex. Note, no hats or anything that covers your head are allowed (must be removed), and no open shoulders or pants and dresses that do not cover the knees. Tripods and video cameras are also not allowed.

You can walk all around the edges of the top area and look over Cambodia from a number of windows.

*Looking over the courtyard to the front gate of Angkor.*

*Central tower on the top section of Angkor Wat Temple.*

*Reclining Buddha in the central tower.*

## Banteay Kdei

**Date:** Late 12<sup>th</sup> century – early 13<sup>th.</sup>
**King:** Jayavarman II, enhanced by Indravarman II.
**Religion:** Buddhism.
**Style:** Angkor Wat and Bayon.
**Time:** ½ hour.
**Importance:** Almost a smaller and less visited Ta Prohm, with good tree growth over a number of structures. A second temple worthy of starring in an Angeline Jolie movie.
**My Impression:** This temple remains on my favorite list, even after seeing a multitude of temples all over Cambodia. I love to sit in the shade on some of the stone blocks and write. As the temple is less visited than Ta Promh with the same rustic feeling, it is a good choice.

**Best Time To Visit:** Early in the morning, or late in the afternoon.
**GPS:** 13°25'47.3"N 103°53'42.1"E. First entrance.
**GPS:** 13°25'48.5"N 103°54'07.2"E. Second entrance that is opposite Srah Srang, and offers a nice view of Srah Srang.

Banteay Kdei (citadel of the cells), is directly opposite Srah Srang, and 4.2km from the Victory gate, outside Angkor Thom City. The temple was built of soft sandstone, with the outer wall enclosing the temple, built with reused laterite stones, and measures 700m x 500m. The innermost enclosure measures 320m x 300m. Much of the temple is in ruin, and lends to the appeal of the temple, coupled with the jungle setting. The temple is believed to have been built over an existing temple, dating from the 10th century. Banteay Kdei itself is believed to have been used as a Buddhist monastery.

## Banteay Samre

**Date:** Mid-12th century.
**King:** Suryavarman II, Yasovarman II.
**Religion:** Hindu.
**Style:** Angkor Wat.
**Time:** 1 hour (includes drive out).
**Entry Fee:** Angkor Pass.
**Importance:** Very good Angkor Wat style temple, with less people visiting it than Angkor Wat Temple, makes it a relaxed visit with good photo opportunity.
**My Impression:** The temple is a short drive outside of the main circuit that runs in the Angkor Park, and takes you through Pradak village that gives you a glimpse of Cambodian life. The temple itself is in stunning condition, and I loved to be able to walk all around the inside of the temple on the walkway.

**Best Time To Visit:** Early in the morning or late afternoon.
**GPS:** 13°26'33.5"N 103°57'32.6"E for temple.

Banteay Samre (the citadel of the Samre), is a smaller Angkor temple, situated 4.5km from the grand circuit road going through East Baray. The temple takes its name from the Samre people that inhabited the area.

Although the temple was dedicated to the Hindu God Vishnu, the lintels and pediments are richly decorated with Buddhist mythological scenes.

Locals tell of a Cucumber King legend associated with the temple. According to the legend, a farmer from the nearby village of Pradak, grew so tasty cucumbers, that the king ordered the farmer to kill anyone that tried to steal the cucumbers. One night the king wanted cucumbers so badly, that he went out himself to get some. The farmer did not recognize the king at night, and killed the king. As the king had no heir, a Royal elephant was decided upon to appoint the new king. The elephant went to the farmer, and knelt in front of the farmer, and the farmer became the new king. The old king was apparently buried at Pre Rup. The royal servants dislike the new king, and he fled to hide in Banteay Samre Temple.

To get to the temple, go along the grand circuit, and take road 810 to the right, 950m after Pre Rup. Follow this road for 4.1km, though Pradak village, and take the turn off to the temple, which is 250m down the side road.

## *Banteay Srei Temple / Citadel of the Women*

**Date:** 967.
**King:** Yajnavarah (King Rajendravarman's counselor).
**Religion:** Hindu.
**Style:** Banteay Srei.
**Time:** 2 to 4 hours.
**Entry Fee:** Angkor Pass.
**Gate Closes:** 5pm.
**Importance:** Exquisite carvings that turn red brown in the rising or setting sun.
**My Impression:** This temple is a must see. I have been here in both the morning and afternoon, and both times are impressive. The detail on the carvings is exquisite. The riverboat ride at the back of the temple complex is also an experience to try out, and the food at the main restaurant is good.
**Best Time To Visit:** Early in the morning or late afternoon.
**GPS:** 13°35'52.6"N 103°57'56.7"E.

Banteay Srei (Citadel of the Women) / Tribhuvanamahesvra (Great Lord of the Threefold World), is situated 20km from where road 810 links up with the grand circuit road in the east baray (same road as going to Banteay Samre). Drive time is about 20 minutes. From town, the temple is 35km and normally takes 45 minutes with traffic.

The temple was built with red sandstone that coupled with the richly carved figures, makes this a must see temple, especially at sunrise or sunset as the sun's rays gives the temple a golden look (most people do sunset after seeing Angkor Wat). There are a number of Khmer shops and restaurants in the complex, as well as a more upmarket restaurant that sells very good food.

When you exit the temple complex at the back, you can turn right, and follow the road a short distance to an observation station. From here, the road continues along a very scenic area, and ends by a rest station than normally has water and drinks, as well as canoes that one can take a river ride in (about $5). Parking for cars and motorbikes are provided, at 1000 Riel.

As this temple is close to Kbal Spean, I suggest you do the two as a day trip. Either go early in the morning and see the temple first, or do Kbal Spean, then stop at Banteay Srei in the afternoon as the sun sets.

Note, there is no ticket office currently here or at Kbal Spean, and you need your Angkor Pass to see either, so do not forget to bring it along, as you will not be able to enter. There was a ticket office, but with the new picture id passes, this one was closed for the time being.

## *Bakong Temple*

**Date:** 881.
**King:** Indravarman I.
**Religion:** Hindu.
**Style:** Bakong.
**Time:** 1 hour.
**Entry Fee:** Angkor Pass.
**Importance:** State temple of King Indravarman I. Large baray with lily flowers. First Khmer temple-mountain.
**My Impression:** Being part of the Roluos group of temples, this temple is a few minutes ride from Siem Reap, on a good road that runs between trees at a point. I love how the temple stands out in the back with the baray filled with lilies in front, as you approach the temple from the road. A lot of the temple and other structures have been restored and are definitely worth visiting.
**Best Time To Visit:** Sunrise and early morning.
**GPS:** 13°20'52.8"N 103°58'26.4"E turn off from national road 6.
**GPS:** 13°20'09.3"N 103°58'35.2"E for temple.

Bakong is a mountain temple, about 14.5km from Siem Reap, along national road 6 towards Phnom Penh. Bakong was the state temple of King Indravarman I, in the capital city King Jayavarman II used before he moved down from the Kulen Mountains. The temple complex measures 900m x 700m, and encloses two moats, with the base of the temple measuring 67m x 65m, and its stop area 20m x 18m.

The inner moat remains filled, and gives spectacular views as one approach the temple from the second turn off, from national road 6. A main attraction of the temple, besides, its size, is the lintels that contain intricate carvings of Naga's and Makara's. 22 brick temples in various states of collapse surround the main temple. A Naga Bridge that crosses the outer moat, has seven headed Naga snakes, on its sides, and is the first examples of a Naga bridge. There are two entry points to the complex, with the one suggested having a small tower close to the entrance.

To reach the complex, travel 12.5km from town, along national road 6 towards Phnom Penh. Take a side road where a signboard directs to the temple, then travel 1.1km down the road, past Preah Ko and the Angkor Miniatures, until you come to a T-junction. You can go either left or right around, both roads pass by and entrance. To see the small temple near the entrance as mentioned before, go left around. The moat will be in front of you at the T-junction, with Bakong temple in the distance.

Note, if you want to see Prei Monti temple, then take the road off national road 6 immediately before this road.

## *Baphuon*

**Date:** 1060.
**King:** Udayadityavarman II.
**Religion:** Hindu.
**Style:** Baphuon.
**Time:** 1 to 2 hours.
**Importance:** State temple of Yasodharapura.
**My Impression:** This is a large temple with steep steps up; however, the view from the top is very rewarding. The top tower is not currently open to be climbed due to loose stone blocks, but may be open in the future after repairs. With the closeness to Bayon temple and the Elephant Terrace, visiting this temple is well worth your time.
**Best Time To Visit:** Anytime for the bas-relief, early in the morning for the East entrance, and sunrise or late afternoon for a view of the surrounding area.

**GPS:** 13°26'37.5"N 103°51'32.5"E for first terraces.

Baphuon Temple (Tower of Bronze), predates Angkor Thom City, and is surrounded by a 425m x 125m sandstone wall. The temple represents Mount Meru, and is higher than Bayon. The temple was the state temple of Yasodharapura the 11th century.

More than 10 chambers are at its base. Bas-reliefs with daily life and forest scenes, carved in small squares, decorate the temple. The best approach is over a 200m long, elevated walkway on the east side, by the Elephant Terrace.

From the top, one has a superb view of Bayon, Phnom Bakheng in the south and Phimeanakas in the north. The temple has five sandstone bases, with the 1st to 3rd bases surrounded by sandstone galleries. Baphuon is the first style where stone galleries with a central tower are found.
The top level has a central sanctuary with two wings, decorated with animated figures (in restoration), visible from the west side at floor level.

After visiting the temple, turn right as you look at the stairs, then go around to the back and through the wall by an archway, to reach Phimeanakas Temple.

## Bayon Temple

**Date:** 1181 ~ 1218.
**King:** Jayavarman VII.
**Religion:** Buddhism.
**Style:** Bayon.
**Time:** 1 to 2 hours.
**Importance:** Bas-reliefs of daily life and war. State temple of Jayavarman VII. 54 towers with impressive multi-direction facing heads with 216 faces. A good view of the surrounding area from the top level.
**My Impression:** The up to 2 ½m faces on the top level is a must see. Although the view of the surrounding area is not as impressive as from Baphuon or Bakong temple, it is still a sight to see. A good time to visit is early in the morning when the sun shines fully onto the faces.
**Best Time To Visit:** Sunrise to early in the morning or late afternoon.
**GPS:** 13°26'28.3"N 103°51'37.5"E.

Bayon Temple (Golden Tower), is in the center of Angkor Thom, and was King Jayavarman VII's state temple. The temple represents Mount Meru, or the center of the universe in Hindu and Buddhist believe. A 72m long, two-level pathway that is guarded by lions, leads to the eastern gate of the temple. Although the temple was originally built as a Buddhist temple, King Jayavarman VIII converted it to a Hindu temple, and destroyed the Buddhist statues. Interestingly, shrines for both Vishnu and Shiva are found at the temple. The temple is richly decorated with reliefs, with religious and mythological scenes found on the inner galleries and war and daily life scenes found on the outer galleries.

Visitors can easily access the 3rd floor by means of stairs, where sculpted faces, believed to be either of Lokeshvara (the Bodhisattva of compassion) or King Jayavarman VII, as large as 2 ½m are found.

Three enclosures are found at the temple. The ground floor holds the 3rd enclosure, and measures 160m long x 140m wide. Daily life, war scenes, and dancing Apsaras can be found here.

The second enclosure is 80m long x 70m wide. Large faces of Lokeshvara, Hindu religious and mythological scenes, as well as sculptings of Buddha can be found here.

The 1st enclosure consists of the 3rd floor, where Hindu images as well as Buddha faces can be found. The circular central sanctuary is surrounded by eight sanctuary towers with sculpted faces. Four satellite sanctuaries surround them, with the Western sanctuary dedicated to Vishnu, the Northern one to Shiva, and Southern sanctuary to the Buddha.

A 3.6m image of a seated and meditating Buddha, on the coiled body of the snake Mucalinda, was discovered in a pit under the Southern sanctuary. This image is now the Buddha image at Wat Prampei Loveng (see Buddha section). A visit in the early morning or afternoon as the sun sets, gives good views over the Angkor Thom area surrounding the temple, as well as the many large faces on the top floor.

A walkway spans all around the top floor, while being surrounded by large towers with faces in all four directions. The center of the top, contains a large temple structure, with the largest tower in the center.

The faces on the top level are up to 2 ½m high. Believe are that they are of either Lokeshvara (the Bodhisattva of compassion) or King Jayavarman VII. The temple is best visited in the early morning or late afternoon, if you want the sun directly on the faces, and midday to avoid the crowds if you want wide shots of the top area.

# Chao Say Tevoda

**Date:** End 11th century – early 12th century.
**King:** Suryavarman II, Yasovarman II, Jayavarman.
**Religion:** Hindu.
**Style:** Angkor Wat.
**Time:** ½ hour.
**Importance:** A small Angkor Wat style temple that gives good photo opportunity.
**My Impression:** This compact temple has a lot to offer in its detailed artwork. Somehow, this and Thommanon temple across the road reminds me of a locomotive. Combine a visit here with a visit to Thommanon temple across the road.
**Best Time To Visit:** Early to mid-morning.
**GPS:** 13°26'43.8"N 103°52'40.2"E.

Chao Say Tevoda is 500m from the Victory Gate, outside Angkor Thom City, and directly across from Thommanon. These two temples are often confused as being planned together, but Chao Say Tevoda was built later than Thommanon. They were also not planned to line up with the Victory lane (road leading to the Royal Palace), as this was built later.

# East Mebon

**Date:** 953.
**King:** Rajendravarman.
**Religion:** Hindu
**Style:** Pre Rup.
**Time:** 1 hour.
**Importance:** Impressive lintels of the towers, and the large elephant statues guarding the corners.
**My Impression:** With large trees surrounding the temple, the view from the top in the morning is worth a visit. I liked the open top level, and the large elephant statues.
**Best Time To Visit:** Sunrise to early morning, or late afternoon to sunset.
**GPS:** 13°26'47.8"N 103°55'15.2"E.

East Mebon sits atop a fabricated island, and is not a mountain temple. The confusion comes from the appearance of height, due to the baray being dry. Water would have come up around 5m, around the temple. The temple itself has a laterite base of 126m x 121m, and has five towers on the top level, with a library on each corner of the lower level, with galleries on the first level. Elephant statues stand guard on each corner.

## *Elephant Terrace*

**Date:** late 12<sup>th</sup> century.
**King:** Jayavarman VII.
**Religion:** Buddhism.
**Style:** Bayon.
**Time:** ½ hour.
**Importance:** Elephant sculpting with their trunks almost reaching the ground.
**My Impression:** The terrace is impressively large, with elephant sculpting all along the wall. However, I liked the group of elephants at the far right end of the wall best. This is close by where the Leper King Terrace starts.
**Best Time To Visit:** Sunrise and early in the morning to catch the light shining directly onto the terrace. Just before midday to get the sun on the hidden relief of a five-headed horse.
**GPS:** 13°26'49.8"N 103°51'31.8"E.

The Elephant Terrace (Royal Terrace) forms part of the Eastern boundary of the Royal Palace grounds. It is believed that the king watched processions, parades and other events from the Terraces.

The terrace contains extensive sculpting of Devata's, Apsara's, mythological animals and demons and the terrace got its name from the sculptures of elephants found here, where elephant heads protrude out from the wall, with their trunks forming pillars that extend to the ground. (Similar to those of the gates of Angkor Thom.) Chinese diplomat Zhou Daguan that lived in Cambodia for a year, recorded that the king appeared daily on the terrace, to listen to and address complaints and problems of the citizens of his Kingdom.

There is a hidden relief of a five-headed horse at the north end of the terrace.

## *Leper King Terrace*

**Date:** late 12<sup>th</sup> century.
**King:** Jayavarman VII.
**Religion:** Buddhism.
**Style:** Bayon.
**Time:** ½ hour.
**Importance:** Leper King Statue. Believed to be the terrace where the king watched parades and addressed his people.
**My Impression:** Walking through the passage with all the intricate sculpting makes a visit here worthwhile.
**Best Time To Visit:** Sunrise and early in the morning to catch the light shining directly onto the terrace.
**GPS:** 13°26'50.5"N 103°51'31.7"E.

The Leper King Terrace is 25m long, and directly north of the Elephant Terrace. It is named after the "Leper King" statue that was found here. The statue is believed to be of King Yasovarman I (also known as the Leper King), who suffered from leprosy, although current thought is that the statue might represent Kubera, the god of wealth (also believed to suffer from leprosy), or Yama, the God of death. The original statue is now in Phnom Penh museum, with a copy now decorating the terrace. The terrace is believed to represent Mount Meru, and rows of carved figures of multi headed Naga snakes, armed guardians, Garuda's and female celestial beings, decorate the walls.

# Neak Pean

**Date:** Second half of the 12th century.
**King:** Jayavarman VII.
**Religion:** First Hindu, then later Buddhism.
**Style:** Bayon.
**Time:** ½ to 1 hour.
**Importance:** Unique island temple with a long walkway to it, which is almost level with the water in the wet season. Sculpting of Balaha (mythical Buddhist horse)
**My Impression:** I visited the temple in the wet and dry season, and must say that it is a drastic difference. I loved walking towards the temple early in the morning, with the water almost touching the walkway, and smooth as glass. The hydraulic system in service of Buddhist believe, is something to see.
**Best Time To Visit:** Early in the morning or late afternoon, with the wet season the best time of year. Mid-November to Mid-January.
**GPS:** 13°28'02.5"N 103°53'41.3"E (start of walkway).

Neak Pean (the entwined snakes/ serpents) is a temple situated on an island in the center of Jayatataka baray, a 3,5km long x 900m wide water reservoir. The square temple complex is surrounded by 350m laterite walls, and is reached by a raised, 400m long wooden walkway. Initially a royal Hindu site, then rededicated to Buddha with the addition of the four gargoyles, then later rededicated to Lokeshvara, the Bodhisattva of compassion (believed to possess the powers of healing). Only the central pond and four surrounding ponds remain, and are laid out in the shape of a lotus flower.

The central pond measure 70m x 70m, and symbolizes Lake Anavatapta, a lake located in the center of the world in Buddhist cosmology. The smaller ponds (srah), measure 20m x 20m, and have chapels that link the ponds to the main pond. Each chapel is decorated by a different stone gargoyle in a shape, and are the head of an ox, a lion, an elephant, and a horse. Water flowed down from the central pond, through the gargoyles' open mouths into their corresponding chapel's basins. The water flowing down into the small ponds, symbolize the lake meadows of the Kailash Mountain in the Tibet. The ponds were used by pilgrims to wash away their sins. The central pond has a 14m in diameter stone island that is encircled by two Naga snakes that guard the East and West entrances. The West Nagas' tales are intertwined, and gives the name of the temple complex. Initially, it was Rajyasri (the fortune of the kingdom), as written on a stele at Preah Khan temple. Several lingas of Shiva and Yonis are found around the central sanctuary, and Balaha (a flying horse), is situated by the east entrance. Balaha is said to rescue stranded merchants from the island Singhala, that is inhabited by demons in the form of young women.

# *Phimeanakas*

**Date:** 950 ~ 1050.
**King:** Rajendravarman or Suryavarman I.
**Religion:** Hindu.
**Style:** Kleang.
**Time:** ½ hour.
**Importance:** State temple of Suryavarman I. Smaller version of Koh Ker Temple.
**My Impression:** This small temple is quickly visited. The view over the Royal grounds is worth the climb to the top. The temple sits deeper into the forest, and a walk around the temple towards the Royal pools is worth it.
**Best Time To Visit:** Early in the morning when the sun shines against the temple front as pictured above.
**GPS:** 13°26'44.3"N 103°51'22.1"E.

Phimeanakas Temple (Celestial Palace / the Golden Tower), is a laterite, stepped pyramid temple, located near Baphuon, at the center of the Royal Palace enclosure. The temple was used by King Jayavarman VII as his private temple. Two pools next to the temple may have been used for bathing. The remains of an earlier structure, with inscriptions with dedications to Vishnu, dating to 910, were uncovered here. On the door an inscription dated 1011, reads of an oath of allegiance to the Angkor King. The base measures 35m long x 28m wide, and the upper platform 30m long x 23m wide.

The galleries on top of the pyramid were the first vaulted galleries to be built at Angkor. A stele written by King Jayavarman VII's second wife was found in 1916 by Henri Marchal. The stele tells how the king's first and second wife helped spread Buddhism, as well as a number of important events, including the King's coronation in 1181.

Legend foretells that on top of the temple, lived a spirit in the form of a nine headed snake, who is the Lord of the Khmer Kingdom. The spirit took the form of a woman at night, and the King had to climb to the top of the tower and sleep with the spirit. If he failed in his duty, great disaster would befall the Kingdom, and if the spirit did not show, it foretold the Kings death. The temple as with the Royal Pools and terraces, are best visited in the early morning, when the sun bathes them in golden light.

# *Phnom Bakheng*

**Date:** Dedicated around 907.
**King:** Yasovarman I.
**Religion:** Hindu.
**Style:** Bakheng.
**Time:** 1 to 3 hours (including climbing up).
**Importance:** State temple of the first capital at Angkor. Excellent views of the surrounding area and awesome sunset views.
**My impression:** The walk up to the temple with the vegetation almost hugging you is something to experience. The temple is large and most of it has been restored. The view from the top is a must see. It can get very hot here in the midday, bring water with you. The afternoon elephant ride up to and down from the temple is something to do, or ride from here to Bayon temple in the early morning.
**Best Time To Visit:** Sunrise and early in the morning give good views with normally few people around. Midday gives good photo opportunity of the surrounding landscape. Late afternoon and sunset is worth it, however, at sunset time it can get very crowded here.
**GPS:** 13°25'25.8"N 103°51'34.4"E.

Phnom Bakheng (originally Yasodharapura) is a mountain temple dedicated to Shiva, and located on mountain Bakheng, 400m before the South Gate.

The temple was the state temple of the first city at Angkor. King Yasovarman I, moved the capital from, now Roluos group (Hariharalaya), to here, until 928, when it was abandoned until 968, when King Jayavarman V briefly used it.

The entire hill was surrounded by a moat measuring 650m x 436m, of which parts of it is still visible. In total, there were 108 smaller towers, with 1 large tower overseeing the smaller ones. 108 is considered a sacred number in both Hindo and Buddishm. You can see Angkor Wat, Phnom Krom (South), Phnom Khulen (North) and Phnom Bok from the top, and sunrise and sunset views are splendid from here. There are two ways up to the top, with the side going up on the right, offering views of Prasat Baksei Chamkrong, and the West Baray.

In the afternoon, you can ride an elephant up for $20, and it takes about 15 minutes. The ride down is $15. I suggest you go up on the path that leads up to the right of the mountain, and come down on the one that leads up to the left of the mountain. The temple is very busy in the afternoon with people wanting to get a sunset view of Angkor Wat, although with most cameras you will not be able to see Angkor Wat. If you want the temple mostly to yourself to take splendid pictures of the countryside, come in the heat of the day at around noon.

## *Prasat Baksei Chamkrong*

**Date:** Early to middle 10th century (rededicated in 948).
**King:** Harshavarman I, restored by Rajendravarman.
**Religion:** Hindu.
**Style:** Bakheng to Koh Ker.
**Time:** 20 minutes.
**Importance:** The only pyramid temple at Angkor that was not used by a king as a state temple.
**My Impression:** This small temple is quickly visited. The climb to the top is steep, but the view over the surrounding forest is worth it.
**Best Time To Visit:** Anytime for the temple, but during the morning to see the light to break through the treetops on the East side.
**GPS:** 13°25'30.9"N 103°51'33.6"E.

Prasat Baksei Chamkrong (the bird with sheltering wings) is a stepped pyramid temple, located 280m before the South Gate. The name however is new, and not relevant to the building of the temple. The temple fell into disarray, when the capital moved to Koh Ker, and was restored and rededicated in 948 by King Rajendravarman.

The temple has four tiers, that measure 27 x 27m at the base, to 15 x 15m at the top, with a 13m high tower that measures 8 x 8m at the base. The opening in the tower faces east. This temple is almost a smaller replicate to the main Koh Ker temple.

## *Prasat Kravan*

**Date:** 921.
**King:** High-ranking priest of King Harshavarman I.
**Religion:** Hindu.
**Style:** Bakheng to Koh Ker.
**Time:** 20 ~ 30 minutes.
**Importance:** Unique brick bas-relief. Five brick towers in a single row, normally only three towers.
**My Impression:** This small temple is well restored, and the brick bas-relief makes this a worthwhile visit.
**Best Time To Visit:** Sunrise for the towers, morning to midday for the bas-reliefs.
**GPS:** 13°25'10.7"N 103°53'58.0"E.

Prasat Kravan (the cardamom sanctuary) is a 5-stupa sanctuary, 3km from the back entrance to Angkor Wat Temple, and was dedicated to Vishnu, the Supreme God of Hinduism. The sculptures found inlaid directly in the brickwork of the towers, are unique in Angkor, and more found in Cham temples in Vietnam.

This is the only temple in Angkor that features artwork that stands out of the brickwork. An extensive restoration has been completed, with minor restoration ongoing.

## *Prasat Ta Som*

**Date:** Late 12<sup>th</sup> century.
**King:** Jayavarman VII, enlarged by Indravarman II.
**Religion:** Buddhism.
**Style:** Bayon (3<sup>rd</sup> period).
**Time:** ½ hour.
**Importance:** Large tree growing over the entrance:
**My Impression:** I love the way the tree embraces the entrance. It took me two visits to find it, as the tree is actually the last entrance to the temple, on the far side of the grounds. Thus, you have to walk all the way through the grounds to get to it. Now you know.
**Best Time To Visit:** Early morning or late afternoon.
**GPS:** 13°27'52.1"N 103°54'42.9"E.

Prasat Ta Som is 7km from the North Gate, and a small temple complex of 240m x 200m wide, and is most famous for the tree growing over the back entrance. Ta Som was dedicated to King Jayavarman's ancestors. Both the East and West gopura entrances of the laterite outer enclosure have large faces of Lokeshvara, the Bodhisattva of compassion, that face in all four directions. The temple itself is oriented towards the East, and has three enclosures and a moat surrounding a single sanctuary tower in the center of the temple. Although dedicated to Buddha, the lintels and pediments contain sculpting of Hindu depictions that was added later. To get to the famous tree over the entrance, walk directly through the entire complex to the back.

## *Preah Khan / Kompong Svay*

**Date:** 1191 (for city, original complex early 11th century).
**King:** Jayavarman VII, with alterations by Jayavarman VIII.
**Religion:** Buddhism later changed to Hindu.
**Style:** Bayon.
**Time:** 1 to 3 hours.
**Importance:** Ta Prohm atmosphere, on a larger scale. Unique round columned, two-story building (pictured above).
**My Impression:** The temple with its rustic feel makes an impression, especially late afternoon when this building is lit in the setting sun's rays. A third temple that could feature in another Angelina Jolie movie.
**Best Time To Visit:** Anytime for the complex, with late afternoon being best for the NE building pictured above.
**GPS:** 13°28'01.5"N 103°52'40.6"E.

Preah Khan, (City of the Sacred Sword), is located just outside Angkor Thom City, approximately 2km after the Northern Gate, and was a small city itself, as well as a Buddhist university. From a stele it is known that close to 100,000 people were dedicated to serve this complex. It is thought that the complex may have been the palace of Yasovarman II and Tribhuvanadityavarman.

References indicate that a major battle against the Chams occurred here when Angkor was retaken, and that the Cham king may have died here. Preah Khan was dedicated to Dharanindravarman, Jayavarman VII's father. A moat, measuring 800m x 700m, surrounds the complex, and gives some of the best water views when approaching the temple.

There are three entrances in use, and I recommend the one directly off Banteay Prei and Prasat Prei, where the toilets are. There are a great number of buildings to see here, as well as trees growing over the walls and structures, in the same manner as Ta Prohm.

Many of the Buddhist figures had been destroyed and replaced by Hindu figures by King Jayavarman VIII in the 13th century.

# *Pre Rup*

**Date:** 961.
**King:** Rajendravarman.
**Religion:** Hindu.
**Style:** Banteay Srei.
**Time:** ½ hour to 1 hour.
**Importance:** Large brick towers on the top level. Good artwork still visible on the lintels. Mixture of brick, laterite, and sandstone used to good effect. Very good views from the top level.
**My Impression:** The view from the top is worth the visit alone, however, combined with the large towers and mixture of building materials, this is a must see.
**Best Time To Visit:** Sunrise to early morning, and late afternoon to sunset.
**GPS:** 13°26'06.0"N 103°55'17.2"E.

*Anton Swanepoel*

The Pre Rup (change the body/ enlightenment) was the state temple of King Rajendravarman. The temple is 7.9km from the start of the grand circuit, and has several towers, with the central tower containing a sanctuary room. The lintels contain Indra riding the elephant Airavata, Vishnu on Garuda (a large mythological bird, the mount of Vishnu), and other scenes. The temple complex is 127m x 117m large.

# *Royal Pools*

*First pool, the second is directly across from this view. Dec 2014, 7Am.*

**Date:** Late 12th century ~ early 13th century.
**King:** Jayavarman VII.
**Style:** Bayon.
**Time:** ½ hour.
**Importance:** Royal bathing pool for King Suryavarman I.
**My Impression:** I love how the trees reflect on the water. The second pool has an even better view than the first.
**Best Time To Visit:** Early in the morning to catch the reflection of the trees on the water.
**GPS:** 13°26'48.6"N 103°51'28.2"E.

*Anton Swanepoel*

The Royal Pools are around 200m from Phimeanakas temple, and consist of two large pools in series, that are behind a wall that runs between them and Phimeanakas temple. The pools always contain water, but in the rainy season, the pools are at capacity, and can make for some stunning scenic shots early in the morning or late in the afternoon when the sun hits the pools at an angle.

# Ta Prohm

**Date:** Late 12ᵗʰ century – early 13ᵗʰ century.
**King:** Jayavarman VII.
**Religion:** Buddhism.
**Style:** Bayon.

*Anton Swanepoel*

**Time:** 1 to 3 hours.

**Importance:** It is the Angeline Jolie temple! Okay and it has a large tree growing over a temple that made it in a movie. Actually, the temple has a number of large trees, with one that looks like an anaconda that grows over the temple structure.

**My Impression:** The temple itself is worth the visit with its rustic atmosphere, and then add to that the large tree pictured above, another that its roots looks like an anaconda sliding over the wall, and another that its roots grow over an opening, and you have the perfect setting for a movie.

**Best Time To Visit:** Early in the morning to avoid the crowds, or late afternoon when everyone heads to Phnom Bakheng.

**GPS:** 13°26'05.3"N 103°53'06.6"E. Suggested entrance.

Ta Prohm is outside the SW corner of the East baray, and 2.5km from the Victory Gate of Angkor Thom City. The temple was dedicated to Prajnaparamita, King Jayavarman VII's mother, and is now known as the 'Angelina Jolie Temple' that featured in the movie, Tomb Raider, where Angelina played Lara Croft. This fame from the movie, coupled with the attractive jungle setting, makes it one of the most visited temples in the park.

A stele, dated 1186, and written in ancient Sanskrit language, was found here, and was a treasure trove of information about products used for religious ceremonies, the mention of the 102 hospital chapels, the number of priests and people living at Ta Prohm, as well as mention of 121 rest houses across the empire that spread as far away as Phimai in Thailand and the Kingdom of Champa in present day Vietnam. From inscriptions, it was noted that over 80 thousand people maintained this complex (villagers and lay people).

As with many other temples, a large moat surrounds the temple, and access is by bridges and walkways.

The temple has two entrances, with the one facing Angkor Thom City normally used as starting point. Tuk tuk drivers normally drop you off at one entrance, and pick you up at the other. There are more than just one tree growing over the walls of the temple, however, if you want to get a picture without 20 thousand other visitors in the shot, then either go early in the morning (around 7 to 8am, or late in the afternoon, around 4pm).

# *Thommanon*

**Date:** Early 12th century.
**King:** Suryavarman II.
**Religion:** Hindu.
**Style:** Angkor Wat.
**Time:** ½ hour.
**Importance:** Good Angkor style artwork. Small, compact temple.
**My Impression:** I like this temple more than Chao Say Tevoda across the road; however, both are still favorites of mine. As Chao Say Tevoda, this compact temple has a lot to offer in its detailed artwork. Both temples remind me of a locomotive. Combine a visit here with a visit to Chao Say Tevoda temple across the road.
**Best Time To Visit:** Early to mid-morning.
**GPS:** 13°26'48.6"N 103°52'39.4"E.

Thommanon is 500m from the Victory Gate, outside Angkor Thom City, and directly across from Chao Say Tevoda. As mentioned under Chao Say Tevoda, the temples were not built at the same time.

Thommanon temple is the purest Angkorian style dedicated to Brahmanism. It is believed the temple was built at the time when work on Angkor Wat was started.

## *Itinerary*

Here are some suggestions if you are at a loss of what to see on a short time frame.

**Day 1**:
Sunrise at Angkor Wat Temple, then view the reflection of the temple in one of the side pools in front of the temple, and then head to the top tower. Head to the Elephant and Leper King terraces before 9:30 (preferably 8:30) to see the sun reflected on them, then see Baphuon temple, Phimeanakas temple and Royal pools, then head over to Bayon temple, then for a sunset head over to Phnom Bakheng while making a stop at the South Gate and a stop at Prasat Baksei Chamkrong.

**Day 2:**
Sunrise at Srah Srang, then head over to Ta Prohm (be there early to avoid the crowds), then head to Ta Keo followed by the Victory gate. View the North and South Khleang group as well as the Prasat Suor Prat and the Preah Pithu Group. Make it to Preah Khan by 2pm, then from there head to Ta Som, then do a sunset at Angkor Wat temple.

**Day 3**: Option A:
Sunrise at Banteay Srei temple, then see Banteay Samre, head to East Mebon, then to Neak Pean, go through the North Gate, then the Victory gate, and see Thommanon and Chao Say Tevoda, followed by any smaller temples of your liking.

**Day 3**: Option B:
Sunrise at Bakong temple in the Roluos group, then do Prei Monti and Preah Ko, followed by Banteay Samre, East Mebon, then to Neak Pean. If time allows, see Thommanon and Chao Say Tevoda, then a sunset at Banteay Srei. Do allow for about 25 minutes ride from inside Angkor Park to Banteay Srei.

Thank you for taking the time to read *Angkor Wat 20 Must See Temples*.

If you enjoyed this book or found it useful, I would be very grateful if you would please post a short review because your support really does make a difference. Alternatively, consider telling your friends about this book because word of mouth is an author's best friend and much appreciated.

*Anton Swanepoel*

If you want to contact me personally, send me an email @ anton@antonswanepoelbooks.com

*Anton Swanepoel*

# *Map*

The map on the next two pages is a limited view of the Angkor Archaeological Park. You can download a digital copy here (1mb). *http://bit.ly/angkorsmall*

### *Extended Map*

You can download a digital copy of an extended map showing the locations of the Roluos Group Temples and a few others.

**Extended Map Low Resolution (4mb)**
*http://bit.ly/angkorlow*

**Extended Map Low High Resolution (10mb)**
*http://bit.ly/angkorhigh*

You may print the maps for personal use, but may not share or reuse the map, nor use it for any commercial purpose.

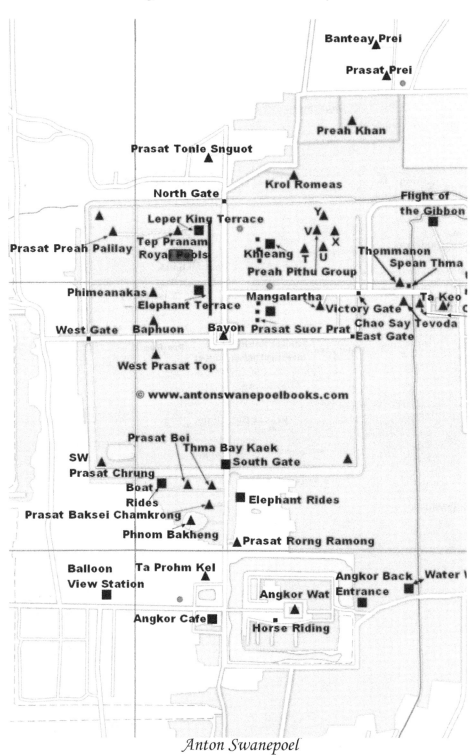

© www.antonswanepoelbooks.com

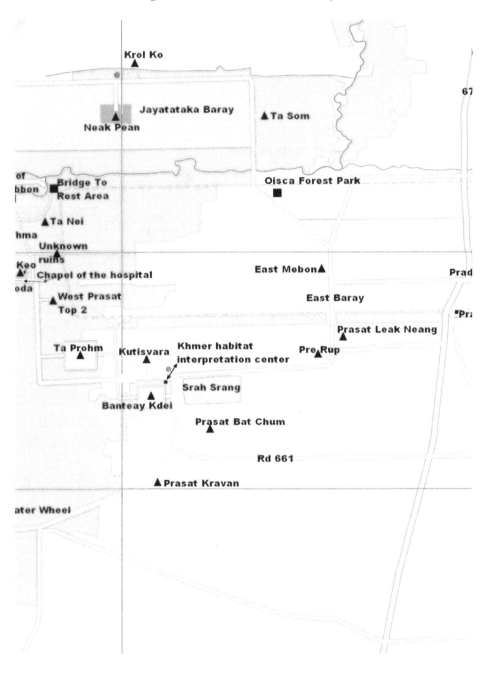

*Anton Swanepoel*

## *About the Author*

As a Technical Diving Instructor and Cave Diver with over seven years' experience working in different places, including the Cayman Islands, I have come to believe that limits are what you set for yourself. I used to be afraid of water until I forced myself into a diving course, and then things just kept going and the thing I feared gave me what I dreamed of doing, travel. Having dived to over 400ft on open circuit, I realize how much of life we miss if we let fear run our life.

Sometimes, life is like a dark tunnel that feels like it is going to squeeze the life from you. However, if you just keep going, you are bound to come out the other side. I love writing, travel, diving, caves, motorcycles, and speed, but as a Reiki Master Teacher, I know you have to balance your life with love, and compassion. Be proud to stand firm in your quest for your dreams, but humble enough to ask for help in reaching them.

*Anton Swanepoel*

# More Books by Anton

## Novels
*Laura and The Jaguar Prophecy (Laura Book 1)*
*Laura and The God Code (Laura Book 2)*
*Untamed Love (Aurora Book 1)*
*The Path To True Love (Aurora Book 2)*

## Travel Diary
*Almost Somewhere*

## Peru Travel
*Machu Picchu: The Ultimate Guide to Machu Picchu*
*Machu Picchu Journals*

## Travel Tips
*Angkor Wat & Cambodia*
*100 International Travel Tips*
*Backpacking SouthEast Asia*

## Motorbike Travel
*Motorcycle: A Guide Book To Long Distance And Adventure Riding*
*Motorbiking Cambodia & Vietnam*

## Cambodia Travel
*Cambodia: 50 Facts You Should Know When Visiting Cambodia*
*Angkor Wat: 20 Must See Temples*
*Angkor Wat Temples*
*Angkor Wat Archaeological Park*
*Angkor Wat Journals*
*Battambang: 20 Must See Attractions*
*Bokor National Park*
*Kampot, Kep and Sihanoukville*
*Kampot: 20 Must See Attractions*
*Koh Ker Temple Site*

*Kulen Mountain & Kbal Spean*
*Phnom Penh: 20 Must See Attractions*
*Preah Vihear Temple*
*Siem Reap: 20 Must See Attractions*
*Sihanoukville: 20 must See Attractions*
*Shopping In Siem Reap*
*Kep: 10 Must See Attractions*

## South African Travel
*South Africa: 50 Facts You Should Know When Visiting South Africa*
*Pretoria: 20 Must See Attractions*
*The Voortekker Monument Heritage Site*
*The Union Buildings*
*Freedom Park*
*The Cradle of Humankind Heritage Site*

## Vietnam Travel
*Ha Long Bay*
*Phong Nha Caves*
*Saigon to Hanoi*
*The Perfumed Pagoda*
*Vietnam: 50 Facts You Should Know When Visiting Vietnam*
*Vietnam Caves*

## Thailand
*Thailand: 50 Facts You Should Know When Visiting Thailand*
*Bangkok: 20 Must See Attractions*
*Ayutthaya: 20 Must See Attractions*
*The Great Buddha*

## Laos
*Vientiane: 20 Must See Attractions*

## Diving Books
*Deep and Safety Stops, and Gradient Factors*
*Dive Computers*
*Diving Below 130 Feet*
*Gas Blender Program*
*Open Water*
*The Art of Gas Blending*

*Anton Swanepoel*

## Writing Guide Books

*How To Format and Publish a Book*
*Supercharge Your Book Description (Grab Attention and Enhance Sales)*

## Self Help Books

*Ear Pain*
*Sea and Motion Sickness*

Made in the USA
Las Vegas, NV
16 August 2023

76201420R00066